EYEWITNESS BOOKS

BOAT

"Jolly Roger"
pirate flag

South American reed raft

19th-century Dutch canal boat

Ship's wheel

Portuguese "half moon"
fishing boat

18th-century Delftware figure
of sailor's farewell

Life jacket

EYEWITNESS BOOKS

BOAT

Ship's bell

Written by
ERIC KENTLEY

Chinese junk
from Foochow

Three-island tramp steamer

Bark in a bottle

Commemorative plate showing
ship launch

ALFRED A. KNOPF • NEW YORK

River boat propeller

Compass card from a
19th-century Russian ship

French ship's
figurehead

River paddle
steamer

![DK]
A DORLING KINDERSLEY BOOK

Project editor Scott Steedman
Art editor Martin Atcherley
Senior editor Helen Parker
Senior art editor Julia Harris
Production Louise Barratt
Picture research Deborah Pownall
Special photography James Stevenson and Tina Chambers
of the National Maritime Museum, London

This is a Borzoi Book published by Alfred A. Knopf, Inc.

This Eyewitness Book has been conceived by Dorling
Kindersley Limited and Editions Gallimard

Manufactured in Singapore
0 9 8 7 6 5 4 3 2

Library of Congress Cataloging in Publication Data
Kentley, Eric.
Boat / written by Eric Kentley.
p. cm. — (Eyewitness books)
Includes index.
Summary: A history of the development and uses of boats,
ships and rafts, from birch-bark canoes to luxury liners.
1. Ships—History—Juvenile literature. 2. Navigation—
History—Juvenile literature. 4. Ships—History—Pictorial
works—Juvenile literature. 5. Navigation—History—
Pictorial works—Juvenile literature. 6. Boats and
boating—History—Pictorial works—Juvenile literature. [1.
Ships—History. 2. Boats and boating—History.] I. Title.
V109.K46 1992 623.8—dc20 91-53136
ISBN 0-679-81678-X
ISBN 0-679-91678-4 (lib. bdg.)

Color reproduction by Colourscan, Singapore
Printed in Singapore by Toppan

Shop sign of a midshipman
with a quadrant

Training dingy

Contents

Four-masted ship *Wendur*

6
Taking to the water

8
Rafts

10
Skin boats

12
Bark canoes

14
Dugouts and outriggers

16
Plank boats

18
Putting planks together

20
Oarsome power

22
Blowing in the wind

24
Sail style

26
The Age of Sail

30
Thar' she blows!

32
A splash of color

34
In sheltered waters

36
Steam and paddle wheels

38
Turn of the screw

40
Last days of the merchant sail

42
Hook, line, and sinker

46
Building in iron and steel

48
Tramping the seas

50
In the dock

52
On the bridge

54
Luxurious liners

58
S.O.S. (Save Our Souls!)

60
Sailing at speed

62
Learning the ropes

64
Index

Taking to the water

To EXPLORE, TO TRAVEL, to trade, to fish, to fight, or just to have fun – people take to the water for all these reasons. For thousands of years, they have been developing new ways to make travel on the water easier, safer, and faster. The earliest craft were simple rafts and floats. But then the hollow shell that sat on the water – probably a hollowed log – was invented. This was the boat, an invention as important as the wheel. Still used all over the world, the wooden boat is the ancestor of the great sailing ships and the huge ferries and container ships of today. There are now many hundreds of different types of boat and ship, made from every material imaginable, from reeds and animal skins to plastic, fiberglass, iron, and steel.

ASSYRIAN AMPHIBIAN
This ancient Assyrian is literally floating on air. He is sitting astride an animal skin that has been blown up with air to make a simple float. The Assyrians were using log rafts, boats made from animal skins (pp. 10–11), and floats like this one for fishing, crossing rivers, and transporting wood at least 2,600 years ago.

WHAT IS A SHIP?
All large vessels are usually called ships, but this word also has a precise meaning. A ship has three or more masts all rigged with square sails. The *Kruzenshtern's* fourth mast has fore-and-aft sails (pp. 24–25), which makes her a "bark," not a ship.

FALLING OFF A LOG
Thousands of years ago, a floating log may have given someone the idea of making the first floating craft. This boy on a log is punting – standing up and pushing a pole against the bottom of the river or lake. But even in the calmest water, the log's shape will make it roll, throwing the boy off. It can be made stable by tying another log to it to form a raft. Or the log can be hollowed out, to make a boat. A boat is more stable because the weight of the passenger is lower in the water.

FLOATING TENDER
There is no clear distinction between a boat and a ship. A rough guideline to go by is that a boat can be put on a ship, but a ship cannot be put on a boat. This is a "tender," a small boat used to ferry people and goods between a ship (or a bigger boat) and the shore. This tender is made of wood planks, though boats can be made from anything that can be formed into a hollow shell.

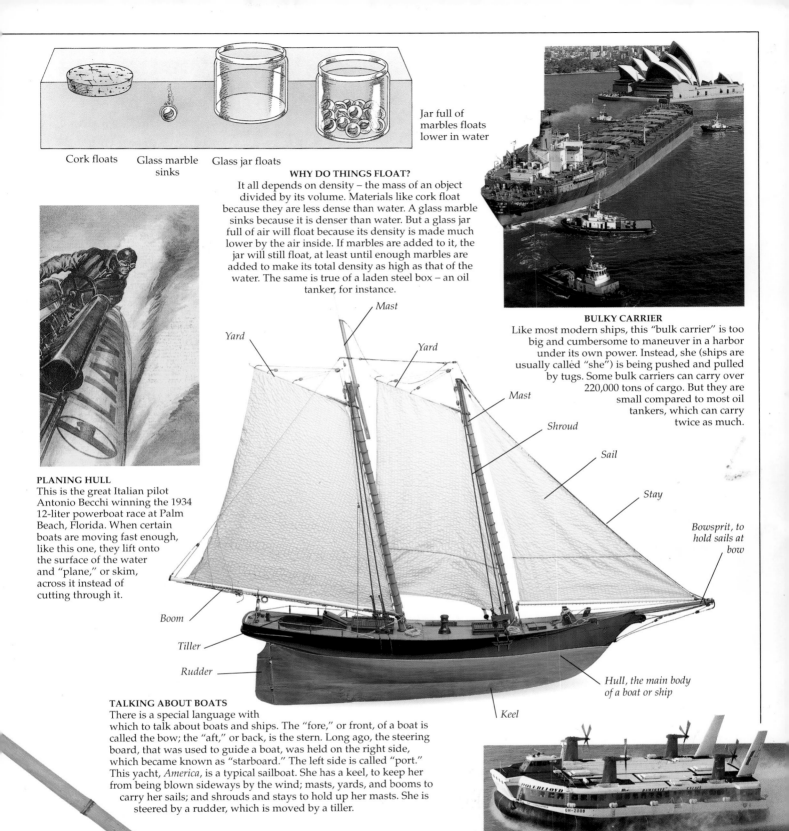

Jar full of
marbles floats
lower in water

Cork floats   Glass marble   Glass jar floats
                  sinks

WHY DO THINGS FLOAT?

It all depends on density – the mass of an object
divided by its volume. Materials like cork float
because they are less dense than water. A glass marble
sinks because it is denser than water. But a glass jar
full of air will float because its density is made much
lower by the air inside. If marbles are added to it, the
jar will still float, at least until enough marbles are
added to make its total density as high as that of the
water. The same is true of a laden steel box – an oil
tanker, for instance.

BULKY CARRIER

Like most modern ships, this "bulk carrier" is too
big and cumbersome to maneuver in a harbor
under its own power. Instead, she (ships are
usually called "she") is being pushed and pulled
by tugs. Some bulk carriers can carry over
220,000 tons of cargo. But they are
small compared to most oil
tankers, which can carry
twice as much.

PLANING HULL

This is the great Italian pilot
Antonio Becchi winning the 1934
12-liter powerboat race at Palm
Beach, Florida. When certain
boats are moving fast enough,
like this one, they lift onto
the surface of the water
and "plane," or skim,
across it instead of
cutting through it.

Mast
Yard
Yard
Mast
Shroud
Sail
Stay
Bowsprit, to
hold sails at
bow
Boom
Tiller
Rudder
Hull, the main body
of a boat or ship
Keel

TALKING ABOUT BOATS

There is a special language with
which to talk about boats and ships. The "fore," or front, of a boat is
called the bow; the "aft," or back, is the stern. Long ago, the steering
board, that was used to guide a boat, was held on the right side,
which became known as "starboard." The left side is called "port."
This yacht, *America*, is a typical sailboat. She has a keel, to keep her
from being blown sideways by the wind; masts, yards, and booms to
carry her sails; and shrouds and stays to hold up her masts. She is
steered by a rudder, which is moved by a tiller.

WHAT IS NOT A BOAT?

Though it travels across water, a hovercraft is not
a boat or a raft because it does not come into
contact with the water. It sits about 8 in (20 cm)
above the surface on a cushion of air,
with its whirring propellers
pushing air, not water.

Rafts

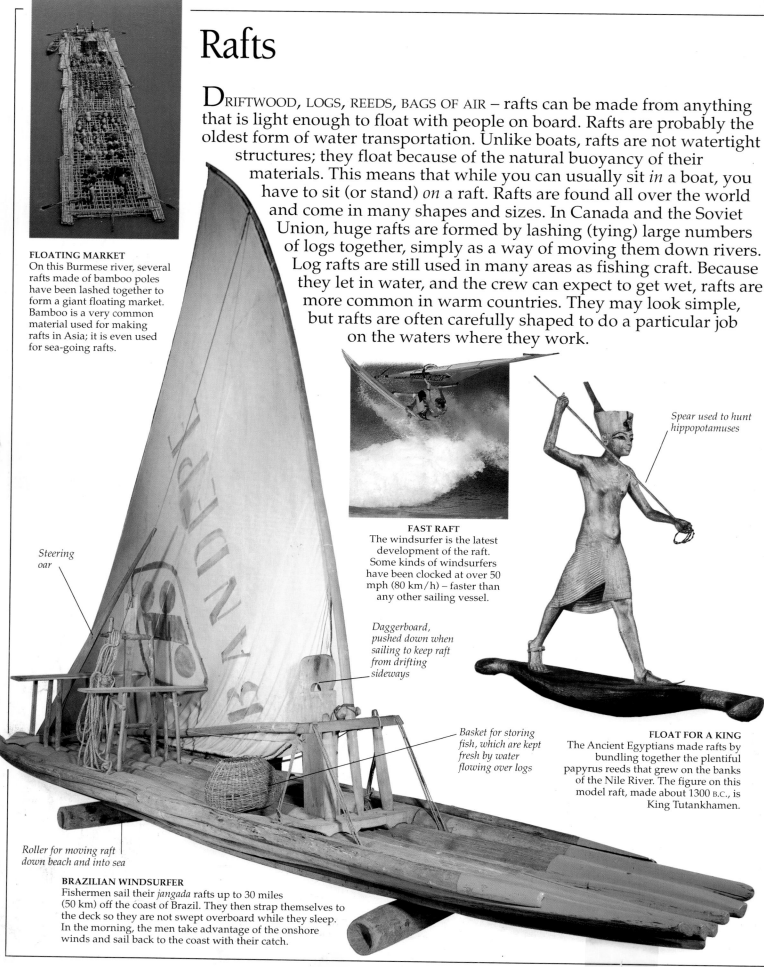

Dᴿɪꜰᴛᴡᴏᴏᴅ, ʟᴏɢꜱ, ʀᴇᴇᴅꜱ, ʙᴀɢꜱ ᴏꜰ ᴀɪʀ – rafts can be made from anything that is light enough to float with people on board. Rafts are probably the oldest form of water transportation. Unlike boats, rafts are not watertight structures; they float because of the natural buoyancy of their materials. This means that while you can usually sit *in* a boat, you have to sit (or stand) *on* a raft. Rafts are found all over the world and come in many shapes and sizes. In Canada and the Soviet Union, huge rafts are formed by lashing (tying) large numbers of logs together, simply as a way of moving them down rivers. Log rafts are still used in many areas as fishing craft. Because they let in water, and the crew can expect to get wet, rafts are more common in warm countries. They may look simple, but rafts are often carefully shaped to do a particular job on the waters where they work.

FLOATING MARKET
On this Burmese river, several rafts made of bamboo poles have been lashed together to form a giant floating market. Bamboo is a very common material used for making rafts in Asia; it is even used for sea-going rafts.

Steering oar

FAST RAFT
The windsurfer is the latest development of the raft. Some kinds of windsurfers have been clocked at over 50 mph (80 km/h) – faster than any other sailing vessel.

Spear used to hunt hippopotamuses

Daggerboard, pushed down when sailing to keep raft from drifting sideways

Basket for storing fish, which are kept fresh by water flowing over logs

FLOAT FOR A KING
The Ancient Egyptians made rafts by bundling together the plentiful papyrus reeds that grew on the banks of the Nile River. The figure on this model raft, made about 1300 B.C., is King Tutankhamen.

Roller for moving raft down beach and into sea

BRAZILIAN WINDSURFER
Fishermen sail their *jangada* rafts up to 30 miles (50 km) off the coast of Brazil. They then strap themselves to the deck so they are not swept overboard while they sleep. In the morning, the men take advantage of the onshore winds and sail back to the coast with their catch.

LIFE RAFT
The Raft of the Medusa, by the 19th-century French painter Théodore Géricault, illustrates a sad tale. When the ship *Medusa* was grounded, 150 people escaped on a huge makeshift raft. But they had few provisions, and they fought among themselves. Only 15 were still alive when the raft was rescued 13 days later.

Lugsail made from reeds

Bipod or "double" mast

HIGH AND DRY
This raft's high, domed shape allows its sailor to kneel well above the cold waters of Lake Titicaca.

THIS IS NOT A BOAT
Although it is shaped like a boat, this fishing raft from Angola clearly lets in water. The light wooden poles are held together with pins and lashings. The raft's shape ensures that when the raft is launched or landed through the surf its fishing gear is not swept overboard.

TITICACA RAFT
Lake Titicaca in the Andes mountains is 12,000 ft (3,500 m) above sea level. As no trees grow at this height, and wood must be carried up the mountains, the local Indians make rafts from reeds that grow in the lake. These elegant craft have hardly changed since they were first seen by Spanish explorers in the 16th century.

WHITE-WATER "RAFTS"
Like rafts made from inflated animal skins or bladders (p. 6), the craft used in the sport of white-water "rafting" float with the help of trapped air. But they are watertight and are therefore not really rafts but boats.

KON TIKI
In 1947 the Norwegian Thor Heyerdahl sailed this balsa raft 4,000 miles (6,500 km) across the Pacific Ocean in an attempt to show that South Americans could have colonized Polynesian Islands.

Skin boods

Wᴿᴬᴾᴾᴱᴰ ᴬᴿᴼᵁᴺᴰ ᴬ ᴸᴵᴳᴴᵀ ᵂᴼᴼᴰᴱᴺ ᶠᴿᴬᴹᴱᵂᴼᴿᴷ, the hide of an animal makes a watertight boat. All kinds of animal skins are used for this purpose. In India, round boats called paracils are built using buffalo hides; in Tibet, sailors are kept dry thanks to the hides of yaks (wild ox). The native people of the North American prairies once crossed rivers in "bull boats," which were wrapped in bison hide. The Inuit (Eskimos) of the Arctic cover their kayaks with sealskins, though with the recent rarity of seals, most have switched to waterproofed canvas. The design of many skin boats has not changed in centuries. They are often made in places where wood is scarce. They are light, maneuverable, and easy to carry, and some are surprisingly safe in wild water.

RAW MATERIALS
In the British Isles, cattle hide was once used to make round boats called coracles. It has since been replaced by canvas or flannel coated with tar.

GOING WITH THE FLOW
The coracle of Wales and England is a one-person boat used for river fishing. The coracler paddles downstream and then has to walk back along the bank carrying the boat on his back.

LIGHT AND SKINNY
Its light framework and cover make the curragh easy to carry from the sea to a safe spot high on the beach.

IRISH SEABOAT
The curragh is used by people who live on the western coast of Ireland, where trees are few and the Atlantic surf is wild. It is built from cattle hides – or in this case, a modern substitute, canvas – stretched over a willow frame. Despite its fragile appearance, the curragh is used for sea fishing and for transportation to islands far from the mainland.

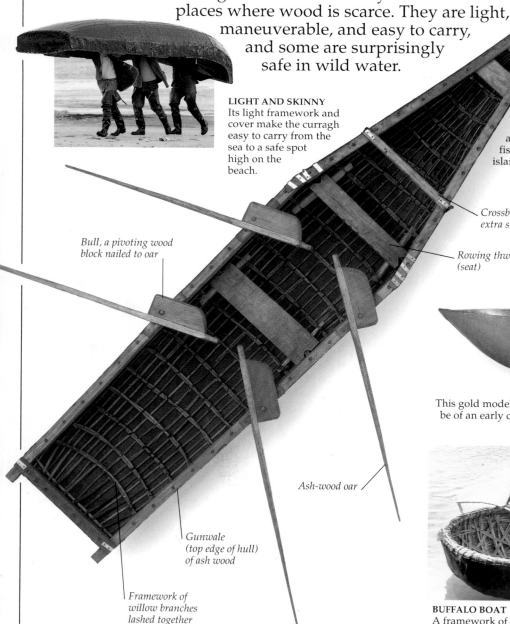

Bull, a pivoting wood block nailed to oar

Crossbeam for extra strength

Mast

Rowing thwart (seat)

Steering oar

Ash-wood oar

Gunwale (top edge of hull) of ash wood

Framework of willow branches lashed together

BURIED TREASURE
This gold model, found in a buried cache in Ireland, may be of an early curragh. It dates from the 1st century B.C.

BUFFALO BOAT
A framework of interwoven slats of split bamboo makes the south Indian paracil strong and rigid. It is covered with several buffalo hides sewn together.

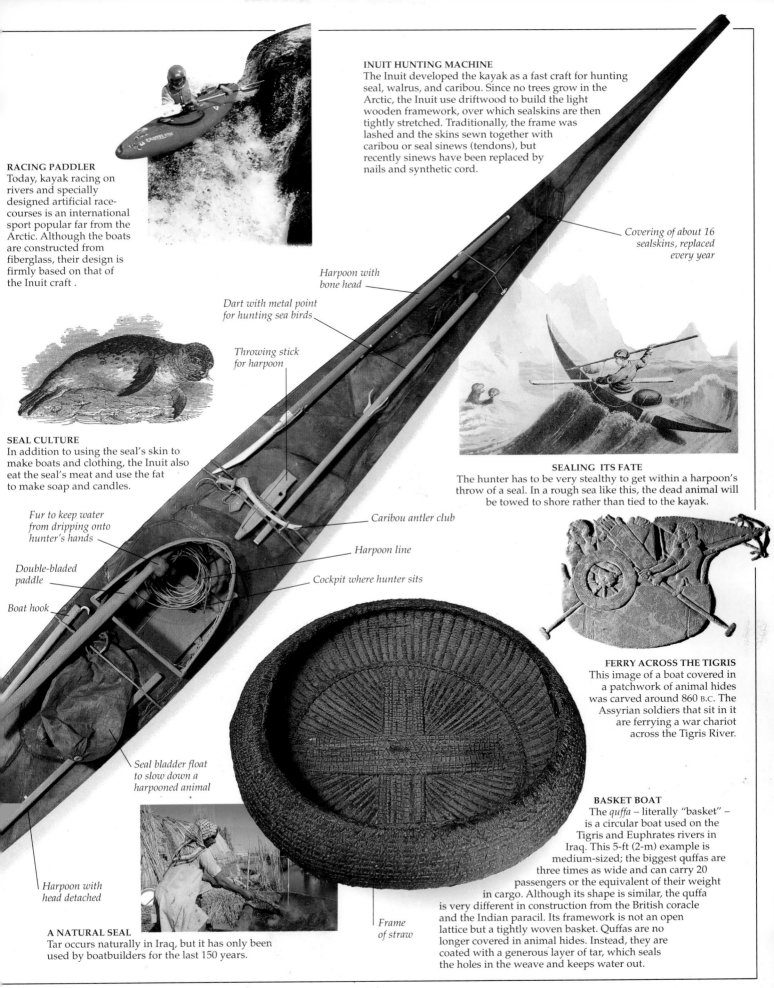

RACING PADDLER
Today, kayak racing on rivers and specially designed artificial race-courses is an international sport popular far from the Arctic. Although the boats are constructed from fiberglass, their design is firmly based on that of the Inuit craft .

INUIT HUNTING MACHINE
The Inuit developed the kayak as a fast craft for hunting seal, walrus, and caribou. Since no trees grow in the Arctic, the Inuit use driftwood to build the light wooden framework, over which sealskins are then tightly stretched. Traditionally, the frame was lashed and the skins sewn together with caribou or seal sinews (tendons), but recently sinews have been replaced by nails and synthetic cord.

Covering of about 16 sealskins, replaced every year

Harpoon with bone head

Dart with metal point for hunting sea birds

Throwing stick for harpoon

SEAL CULTURE
In addition to using the seal's skin to make boats and clothing, the Inuit also eat the seal's meat and use the fat to make soap and candles.

SEALING ITS FATE
The hunter has to be very stealthy to get within a harpoon's throw of a seal. In a rough sea like this, the dead animal will be towed to shore rather than tied to the kayak.

Fur to keep water from dripping onto hunter's hands

Caribou antler club

Double-bladed paddle

Harpoon line

Boat hook

Cockpit where hunter sits

FERRY ACROSS THE TIGRIS
This image of a boat covered in a patchwork of animal hides was carved around 860 B.C. The Assyrian soldiers that sit in it are ferrying a war chariot across the Tigris River.

Seal bladder float to slow down a harpooned animal

BASKET BOAT
The *quffa* – literally "basket" – is a circular boat used on the Tigris and Euphrates rivers in Iraq. This 5-ft (2-m) example is medium-sized; the biggest quffas are three times as wide and can carry 20 passengers or the equivalent of their weight in cargo. Although its shape is similar, the quffa is very different in construction from the British coracle and the Indian paracil. Its framework is not an open lattice but a tightly woven basket. Quffas are no longer covered in animal hides. Instead, they are coated with a generous layer of tar, which seals the holes in the weave and keeps water out.

Harpoon with head detached

Frame of straw

A NATURAL SEAL
Tar occurs naturally in Iraq, but it has only been used by boatbuilders for the last 150 years.

11

Bark canoes

LIKE THE SKIN of an animal, the skin of a tree – its bark – makes a watertight boat. Bark boats have been made in many places, but they were perfected by the native peoples living in the forests of North America. This land is crisscrossed by a vast network of rivers and lakes which holds half of the fresh water in the world. The people there built canoes for gathering food, hunting, transportation, and waging war. The rivers have many rapids, and bark canoes are strong enough to ride rough water. They are also light enough to be carried around waterfalls and wild stretches of river. The best bark came from the paper birch tree, but some canoes were made of elm, chestnut, and even sticky spruce bark. The Europeans who colonized North America were quick to realize the value of the bark canoe for exploration and the fur trade. At first they imitated the native tradition, though these days the art of building in bark is almost dead. But the shape lives on in thousands of canoes mass produced in plastic and fiberglass.

EUCALYPTUS CANOE
The Aboriginal peoples of Australia made canoes from the bark of the eucalyptus tree. This man is standing in one as he fishes in the coastal waters of Tasmania. Bark canoes were also made in Tierra del Fuego at the tip of South America, and in Africa, China, Indonesia, Siberia, and Scandinavia.

SHOOTING THE RAPIDS
For European colonists and adventurers, the wilderness of Canada offered unrivaled hunting and fishing, as well as the thrill of riding rough water in a light and flexible boat.

ALGONQUIN CANOE
This birchbark canoe was made by the son of an Algonquin chief. The Algonquin lived in the Ottawa Valley and around the many tributaries of the St. Lawrence River, in what is now called Ontario. This is a small canoe, about 9 ft (3 m) long. Algonquin war canoes were up to 35 ft (10.5 m) long. They were much faster than the large elm canoes of the Iroquois, a neighboring people who waged war on the Algonquin.

EXPRESS SERVICE
The Hudson's Bay Company used this 40-ft (12-m) canoe to carry important officials and urgent messages. Among the passengers here is Frances Ann Hopkins, the painter of this picture. The normal rate for paddling such a canoe was 40 strokes a minute.

FINISHING TOUCHES
Unlike skin boats, bark boats are made shell first. This canoe shell is nearly finished. The separate pieces of bark are in place and are being sewn together with spruce roots. When this is done, all the sewing holes will be sealed with spruce gum. Then the supporting ribs will be added, and the canoe will be ready to float.

STIFFENING
A canoe can be made with no more than an ax and a knife. This woman is carving a rib from a piece of spruce. It will be lashed on the inside to stiffen the canoe's bark shell.

WATER-BORNE HUNTERS
The Chippewa, the largest group living in the Great Lakes area, were expert hunters who made canoes for the Hudson's Bay Company. These Chippewa hunters were photographed in about 1900.

Cross-strut to strengthen canoe. It is not a seat – the canoeist sits or kneels on the bottom of the boat

Seam sewn with spruce roots and sealed with spruce gum

ONE PIECE
A bottom view shows that this Algonquin canoe was made from a single piece of bark. Larger canoes were made by sewing on extra sheets.

LIGHT AS A CANOE
This detail from a 17th-century French map shows a "portage" (French for "carrying"). This is a detour in a river journey in which the canoe is carried overland. Early North American traders and travelers had to make regular portages to avoid rapids or to get from one river system to another.

LEGACY OF BARK
The shape of the bark canoe is so suitable for rough water that it is still copied by plank, plastic, and fiberglass boatbuilders today.

A DAY IN THE LIFE OF THE MICMAC
The Micmac lived on the east coast of Canada. Their canoes were closed at the ends so that they could take them to sea and not be swamped by waves. In this scene, painted about 1850, one of the canoes has a sail, an idea (like the guns being used for hunting) taken from European settlers. In earlier times, the Micmac used their canoes to make raids down the coast far to the south.

Dugouts and outriggers

FOR THE LAST 8,000 YEARS, people have been chopping down trees and hollowing them out to make the simplest type of wooden boat – the logboat. The most basic of these "dugout canoes" are roughly made, functional craft large enough to hold only one person standing up. Others, like the war canoes made by the Maoris, the first inhabitants of New Zealand, or by the Haida tribe of Canada's west coast, can carry 20 people and are beautifully decorated. Because they are heavy and sit low in the water, most logboats are restricted to calm waters. However, in the Pacific, logboats were once used for great journeys across the ocean. On some Pacific islands, two or more logboats are lashed together. But more often a wood float is fitted to the side of the dugout hull to make a stable and efficient sailboat – the outrigger canoe.

HOT ROCKS
A hollowed log can be widened by filling it with water that is brought to a boil by tossing in heated stones. The hot water softens the wood so the sides can be pushed apart.

Large mallet

Two-handed adz for rough shaping

WAR CANOE
Using only stone tools, the Maoris of New Zealand created the world's most beautifully carved logboats. Hollowed from kauri pine trees, they were up to 70 ft (22 m) long.

One-handed adz for fine hollowing

Wood peg to fix plank extension to log base

DIGGING OUT
The outside of this Indonesian logboat has been roughly shaped, and the boatbuilder has begun hollowing it out. The depth of the boat is increased by fitting a plank to the top edge of the hull. When the boat has taken shape, the hull will be rubbed with fish skins, which work like sandpaper to give it a smooth finish.

Small mallet for driving in wood pegs

COLORFUL CARGO CARRIER
In Africa and South and Central America, logboats are still an important means of water transportation. Fitted with a rudder and a spritsail or two (p. 24), dugouts like this carry goods around the sheltered waters of Cartagena harbor in Columbia. Similar craft are found in Panama, where they are used for fishing.

Ring to which "painter," or mooring rope, is tied

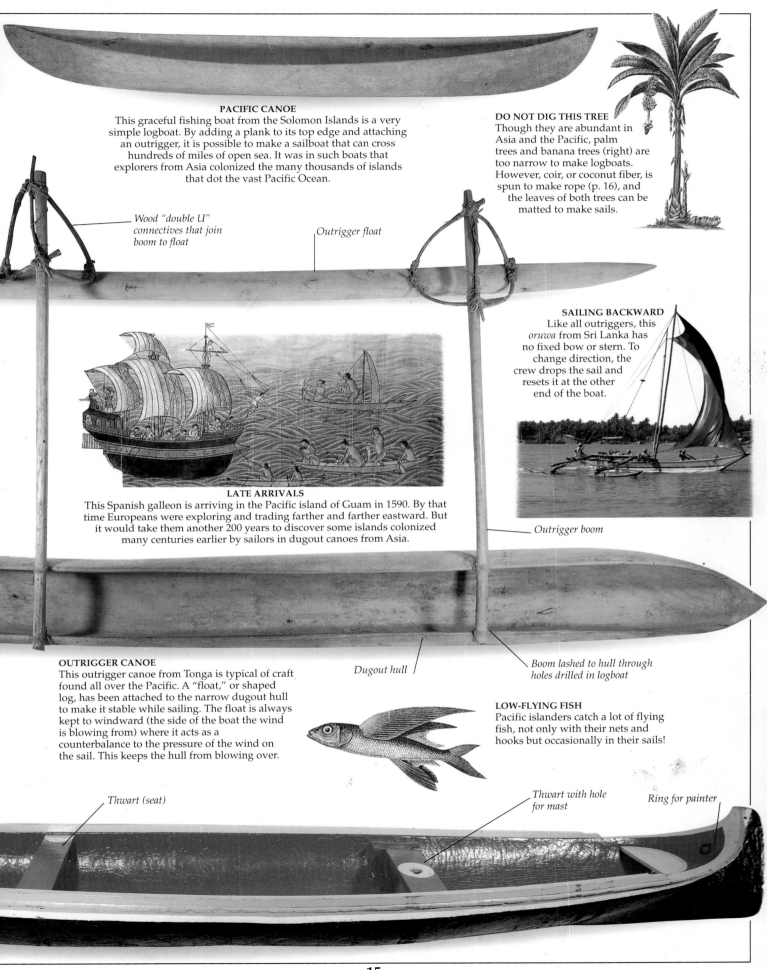

PACIFIC CANOE

This graceful fishing boat from the Solomon Islands is a very simple logboat. By adding a plank to its top edge and attaching an outrigger, it is possible to make a sailboat that can cross hundreds of miles of open sea. It was in such boats that explorers from Asia colonized the many thousands of islands that dot the vast Pacific Ocean.

Wood "double U" connectives that join boom to float

Outrigger float

DO NOT DIG THIS TREE

Though they are abundant in Asia and the Pacific, palm trees and banana trees (right) are too narrow to make logboats. However, coir, or coconut fiber, is spun to make rope (p. 16), and the leaves of both trees can be matted to make sails.

SAILING BACKWARD

Like all outriggers, this *oruwa* from Sri Lanka has no fixed bow or stern. To change direction, the crew drops the sail and resets it at the other end of the boat.

LATE ARRIVALS

This Spanish galleon is arriving in the Pacific island of Guam in 1590. By that time Europeans were exploring and trading farther and farther eastward. But it would take them another 200 years to discover some islands colonized many centuries earlier by sailors in dugout canoes from Asia.

Outrigger boom

Dugout hull

Boom lashed to hull through holes drilled in logboat

OUTRIGGER CANOE

This outrigger canoe from Tonga is typical of craft found all over the Pacific. A "float," or shaped log, has been attached to the narrow dugout hull to make it stable while sailing. The float is always kept to windward (the side of the boat the wind is blowing from) where it acts as a counterbalance to the pressure of the wind on the sail. This keeps the hull from blowing over.

LOW-FLYING FISH

Pacific islanders catch a lot of flying fish, not only with their nets and hooks but occasionally in their sails!

Thwart (seat)

Thwart with hole for mast

Ring for painter

Plank boats

By FIXING SEVERAL PLANKS of wood together, it is possible to build a boat of virtually any shape. A "plank boat" built in this way can be very long and deep; a logboat, on the other hand, can be only as long as the tree it is made from. A plank boat can carry lots of passengers or cargo and sail safely in rough waters. Often, the planks are fastened to a skeleton of sturdy pieces of wood called frames. Alternatively, wood ribs may be inserted after the planks have been fastened together. Some plank boats have no frames or ribs. But most fall into one of two groups: edge-joined, where the planks are fastened edge to edge to form a smooth hull, or lapstrake, where each plank overlaps the one below it.

FLEXIBLE FERRY
Before the building of the harbor of Madras in southeast India, local boats had to brave heavy surf to ferry passengers and cargo to ships anchored offshore. Instead of being nailed, their planks were sewn together to allow them to move as they were battered by the waves.

SEWING BOATS
The fishermen of India's east coast still sew their boats. They place a wad of coir (coconut fiber) or marsh grass between the drilled planks before lacing them together with coir rope.

One-piece frame (rib)

Plank joints coated with resin

Rattan lashing

Lugs

CARVED BOAT
Usually planks are cut straight and then heated and twisted into shape. But each plank of the *tora*, a canoe from the Solomon Islands, has been carved in a precise shape. Rattan – palm fronds (leaves) – are used to sew the planks together. The ribs are then lashed to lugs, wood projections left standing on each plank.

Hand-carved thwart

Bow sheathed with metal

BEASTLY CREW
The Bible says that Noah's Ark, the vessel that saved the animals from the Flood, was 430 ft (133 m) long. In this 13th-century English stained-glass window, it is shown as a hulk, a Northern European planked ship.

Square stern

NOSE IN THE AIR
This edge-joined Portuguese fishing boat is launched from a beach. It has a flat bottom that slides easily over the sand, and a high prow that will never nosedive in rough surf. The square stern is formed by bottom planks that have been curved up sharply. This is a very skilled piece of work – most boats with square sterns are simply fitted with a large board, called a transom.

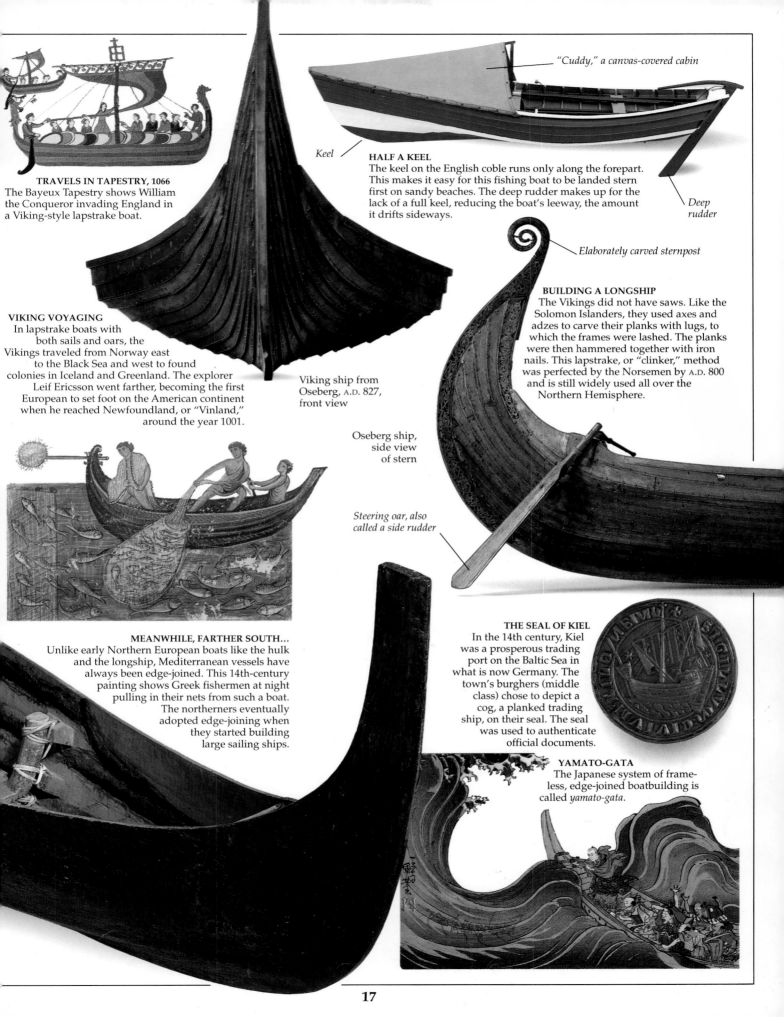

TRAVELS IN TAPESTRY, 1066
The Bayeux Tapestry shows William the Conqueror invading England in a Viking-style lapstrake boat.

"Cuddy," a canvas-covered cabin

Keel

HALF A KEEL
The keel on the English coble runs only along the forepart. This makes it easy for this fishing boat to be landed stern first on sandy beaches. The deep rudder makes up for the lack of a full keel, reducing the boat's leeway, the amount it drifts sideways.

Deep rudder

Elaborately carved sternpost

VIKING VOYAGING
In lapstrake boats with both sails and oars, the Vikings traveled from Norway east to the Black Sea and west to found colonies in Iceland and Greenland. The explorer Leif Ericsson went farther, becoming the first European to set foot on the American continent when he reached Newfoundland, or "Vinland," around the year 1001.

Viking ship from Oseberg, A.D. 827, front view

BUILDING A LONGSHIP
The Vikings did not have saws. Like the Solomon Islanders, they used axes and adzes to carve their planks with lugs, to which the frames were lashed. The planks were then hammered together with iron nails. This lapstrake, or "clinker," method was perfected by the Norsemen by A.D. 800 and is still widely used all over the Northern Hemisphere.

Oseberg ship, side view of stern

Steering oar, also called a side rudder

MEANWHILE, FARTHER SOUTH...
Unlike early Northern European boats like the hulk and the longship, Mediterranean vessels have always been edge-joined. This 14th-century painting shows Greek fishermen at night pulling in their nets from such a boat. The northerners eventually adopted edge-joining when they started building large sailing ships.

THE SEAL OF KIEL
In the 14th century, Kiel was a prosperous trading port on the Baltic Sea in what is now Germany. The town's burghers (middle class) chose to depict a cog, a planked trading ship, on their seal. The seal was used to authenticate official documents.

YAMATO-GATA
The Japanese system of frameless, edge-joined boatbuilding is called *yamato-gata.*

Putting planks together

PLANK MAKING
Until recently, planks had to be cut from logs and boards by hand, with a large saw wielded by two people. Nowadays, they are cut by machines.

ALL PLANK BOATS ARE CONSTRUCTED from a number of flat pieces of wood, each cut to a particular shape. The planks are then twisted and fastened together at their edges. Many wood boats (and all wood ships) are built by first erecting a framework and then nailing on the planks. This "inside-out" method is known as skeleton construction. Some small craft are built the other way around, from the outside in. This is called shell construction. For this method, a template or mold is used to fix the shape of the shell, which is then strengthened with an internal framework. The boat shown here is a small lapstrake craft (p. 16) constructed by the shell method with the help of wood molds.

Shore

Transom

Spall to hold boat to ceiling

Clamp to hold staves in position

Mallet for driving in wedges

Wedge

Wood chain for copying curves in boat

Rib, not yet fully fixed

Shore to hold mold in place

Mold – since boat is symmetrical, only one half is needed

Centerline

BOATBUILDER'S SHED
This boat's stempost and transom (p. 16) are being held in position by spalls, wood struts fastened to the ceiling. The planks on the starboard (right) side have been clamped in position. On the port (left) side, molds are in place for planking up (adding more planks). Once this is complete, one-piece frames, or ribs, will be fastened across the boat.

Mold

MOLDING PLANE
The plane is used to make angled edges on the planks, so that when they are fastened to each other, there is as much contact as possible.

Ball end for flattening nail ends

Small smoothing plane

Copper nails

Marking gauge for scoring (making cuts in) parallel edges

RIVETING STUFF
To fasten two overlapping planks together, holes are drilled through the overlap and nails or rivets (metal pins) are pounded in from the outside. Metal washers – roves – are then driven over the nail points with a roving punch and hammer. Finally, the sharp end is snapped off with pliers and flattened out with the hammer.

Copper roves

Ball-peen hammer

Cutting pliers for snapping off nail ends

Roving punch

Spall

Apron, a timber added to strengthen bow

JIGSAW PUZZLE
A strake is a line of one or more planks which runs from one end of a boat to the other. These nine oddly shaped strakes make up one side of the boat below. Only one of the edges out of all nine strakes is straight – the lower edge of the garboard, the strake that is fastened to the keel. After they are cut, the strakes are put in a steam-filled box. The steam makes them soft and flexible; they are then bent around the molds and fastened one on top of the other.

"Sheer" or top strake

"Garboard" or bottom strake

Sheer strake

Stempost

Keel

Sheer strake

Toe cleat for rowing crutch

Stringer, a horizontal support

Garboard strake

Stempost

Rib

Thwart

Transom

Strongback, which supports keel

Keel

19

Oarsome power

HUMAN MUSCLE POWER is the most obvious and reliable way of driving a boat through the water. Small vessels can be punted (p. 6), or paddled using one paddle held in both hands. Bigger boats may be rowed, with the help of oars that pivot on the side of the boat. Paddles are far more maneuverable, but they are not as efficient as oars. The best way to row is to pull on the oar. But to do this you have to sit with your back to the bow, so you can't see where you are going! The ancient Greeks and Romans built huge oared warships, known as galleys, that were rowed by as many as 1,800 oarsmen; the slaves or prisoners who pulled the oars lived in appalling conditions. Galleys were still being used early in the 19th century.

TIED TO THE MAST
This Roman mosaic tells the legend of how the Greek hero Odysseus eluded the Sirens, sea creatures whose beautiful singing lured sailors to their destruction on the rocks. He made his crew block their ears with wax, though he was too curious to do the same. He had himself tied to the mast so he would not leap overboard when he heard the singing.

Lateen sail for long-distance travel, furled (rolled up) during battles

Fighting platform

Decorated ram

Bronze cannon

Ram

Square sail

Steering oar

Decorated oar blades, each pulled by three men

HARD-NOSED WARSHIP
Greek galleys were floating battering rams. When an enemy ship was spotted, the galley would be rowed into it at full speed, to try to put a hole in it and sink it with the ram, the long projection on the bow. This vase from 510 B.C. shows a small galley with only one bank of oars. The Greeks also built larger "biremes" with two banks of oars and "triremes" powered by three banks.

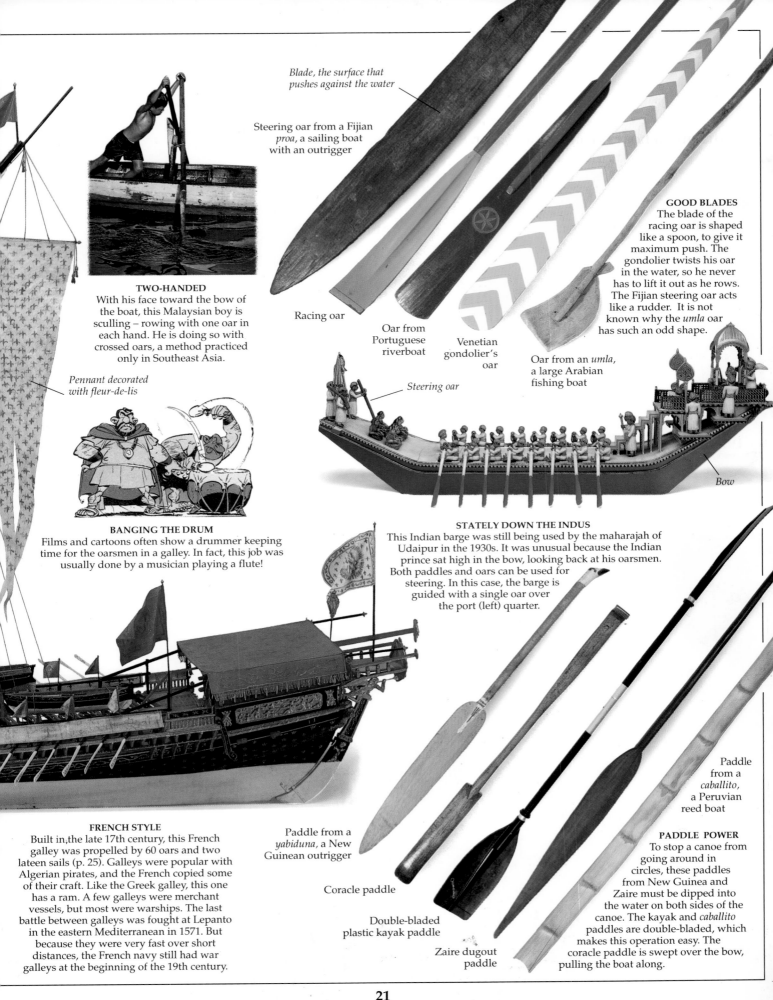

Blade, the surface that
pushes against the water

Steering oar from a Fijian
proa, a sailing boat
with an outrigger

GOOD BLADES
The blade of the
racing oar is shaped
like a spoon, to give it
maximum push. The
gondolier twists his oar
in the water, so he never
has to lift it out as he rows.
The Fijian steering oar acts
like a rudder. It is not
known why the *umla* oar
has such an odd shape.

Racing oar

Oar from
Portuguese
riverboat

Venetian
gondolier's
oar

Oar from an *umla*,
a large Arabian
fishing boat

TWO-HANDED
With his face toward the bow of
the boat, this Malaysian boy is
sculling – rowing with one oar in
each hand. He is doing so with
crossed oars, a method practiced
only in Southeast Asia.

*Pennant decorated
with fleur-de-lis*

Steering oar

BANGING THE DRUM
Films and cartoons often show a drummer keeping
time for the oarsmen in a galley. In fact, this job was
usually done by a musician playing a flute!

STATELY DOWN THE INDUS
This Indian barge was still being used by the maharajah of
Udaipur in the 1930s. It was unusual because the Indian
prince sat high in the bow, looking back at his oarsmen.
Both paddles and oars can be used for
steering. In this case, the barge is
guided with a single oar over
the port (left) quarter.

Bow

Paddle
from a
caballito,
a Peruvian
reed boat

FRENCH STYLE
Built in,the late 17th century, this French
galley was propelled by 60 oars and two
lateen sails (p. 25). Galleys were popular with
Algerian pirates, and the French copied some
of their craft. Like the Greek galley, this one
has a ram. A few galleys were merchant
vessels, but most were warships. The last
battle between galleys was fought at Lepanto
in the eastern Mediterranean in 1571. But
because they were very fast over short
distances, the French navy still had war
galleys at the beginning of the 19th century.

Paddle from a
yabiduna, a New
Guinean outrigger

Coracle paddle

Double-bladed
plastic kayak paddle

Zaire dugout
paddle

PADDLE POWER
To stop a canoe from
going around in
circles, these paddles
from New Guinea and
Zaire must be dipped into
the water on both sides of the
canoe. The kayak and *caballito*
paddles are double-bladed, which
makes this operation easy. The
coracle paddle is swept over the bow,
pulling the boat along.

Blowing in the wind

THE ENERGY OF MOVING AIR can drive a boat through the water. This is called sailing, and people have been doing it for almost as long as they have been making boats. The first sail was probably a hand-held cloth. The next step was to attach it to a mast. Masts are kept upright by standing rigging, consisting of shrouds, which keep the mast from moving sideways, and stays, which keep it from falling forward or backward. The sail itself may be hung from a stay. But usually it hangs from a pole or spar called a yard and is supported at the bottom by another spar, the boom. The sails are controlled by ropes called sheets, which are continually adjusted to keep the sails at the correct angle to the wind.

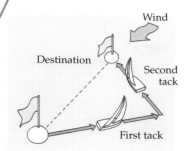

Trapeze wire, which runs between top of mast and harness

TACKY ZIGZAGS
Because it cannot sail straight into the wind, a boat must take a zig-zag course when it heads upwind. This is called tacking. Turning when the wind is behind the boat is known as jibing.

RUNNING WITH THE WIND
How close a boat can sail toward the wind depends on the type of sails it has. But for every boat there is a "no-go zone." The various directions a boat can take in relation to the wind are called the points of sailing. Reaching, for instance, is sailing across the wind.

TRAPEZE ARTIST
To counteract the push of the wind and keep the boat as upright as possible, the helmsman and his crew are leaning out of the windward side of the boat. The crew is standing on the edge of the boat and hanging far out on a trapeze, a harness attached to a wire running to the top of the mast.

Tiller extension

Mainsheet

Shroud

Spreader, to
keep shrouds out
from the mast

"Bermudan" mainsail, a
triangular sail that doesn't
need a top yard because its
forward edge is supported
by the mast

Spinnaker sheet

Centerboard

K 682

Spinnaker, a light,
balloon-like sail used for
speed when on a run or a
broad reach

Spinnaker
sheet

Jib sail

Wind   Wind

Without centerboard   With centerboard
HEELING
A flat-bottomed boat would be blown sideways by
the wind. To keep this from happening, a
centerboard is lowered. The boat then heels – leans
to one side, leeward – instead. Heeling is minimized
in turn by loading the weight of the crew on the
opposite (windward) side. Keels (p. 7),
daggerboards (pp. 8, 63), and leeboards (pp. 34–35)
all have the same effect as centerboards.

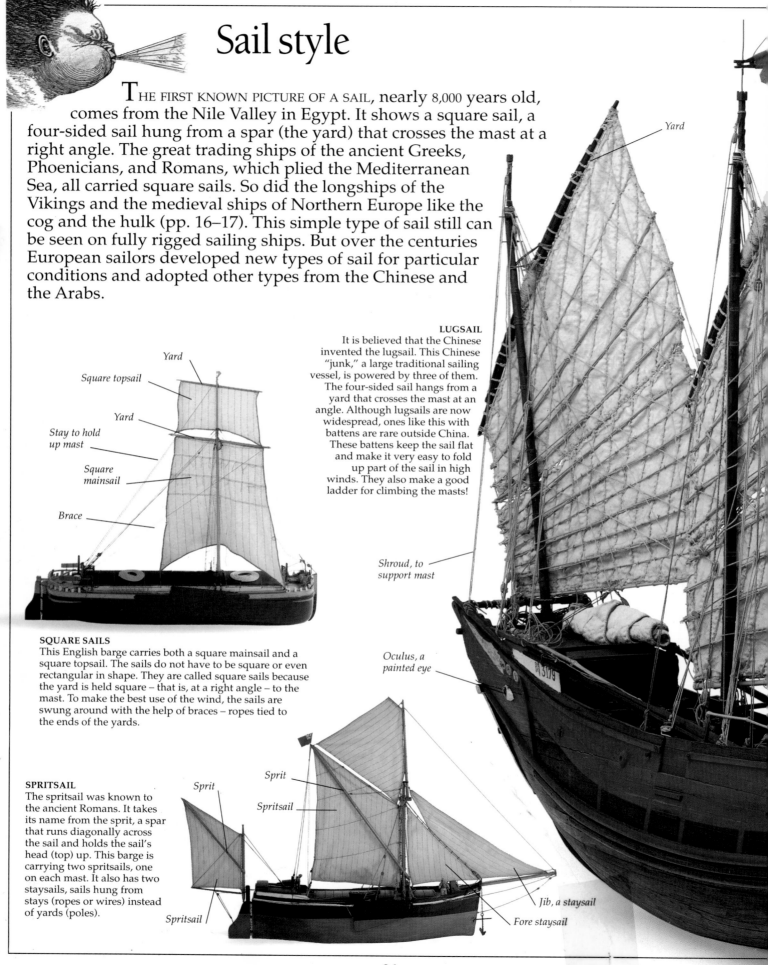

Sail style

THE FIRST KNOWN PICTURE OF A SAIL, nearly 8,000 years old, comes from the Nile Valley in Egypt. It shows a square sail, a four-sided sail hung from a spar (the yard) that crosses the mast at a right angle. The great trading ships of the ancient Greeks, Phoenicians, and Romans, which plied the Mediterranean Sea, all carried square sails. So did the longships of the Vikings and the medieval ships of Northern Europe like the cog and the hulk (pp. 16–17). This simple type of sail still can be seen on fully rigged sailing ships. But over the centuries European sailors developed new types of sail for particular conditions and adopted other types from the Chinese and the Arabs.

Yard

Square topsail

Yard

Stay to hold up mast

Square mainsail

Brace

LUGSAIL
It is believed that the Chinese invented the lugsail. This Chinese "junk," a large traditional sailing vessel, is powered by three of them. The four-sided sail hangs from a yard that crosses the mast at an angle. Although lugsails are now widespread, ones like this with battens are rare outside China. These battens keep the sail flat and make it very easy to fold up part of the sail in high winds. They also make a good ladder for climbing the masts!

Yard

Shroud, to support mast

Oculus, a painted eye

SQUARE SAILS
This English barge carries both a square mainsail and a square topsail. The sails do not have to be square or even rectangular in shape. They are called square sails because the yard is held square – that is, at a right angle – to the mast. To make the best use of the wind, the sails are swung around with the help of braces – ropes tied to the ends of the yards.

Sprit

Sprit

Spritsail

SPRITSAIL
The spritsail was known to the ancient Romans. It takes its name from the sprit, a spar that runs diagonally across the sail and holds the sail's head (top) up. This barge is carrying two spritsails, one on each mast. It also has two staysails, sails hung from stays (ropes or wires) instead of yards (poles).

Spritsail

Jib, a staysail

Fore staysail

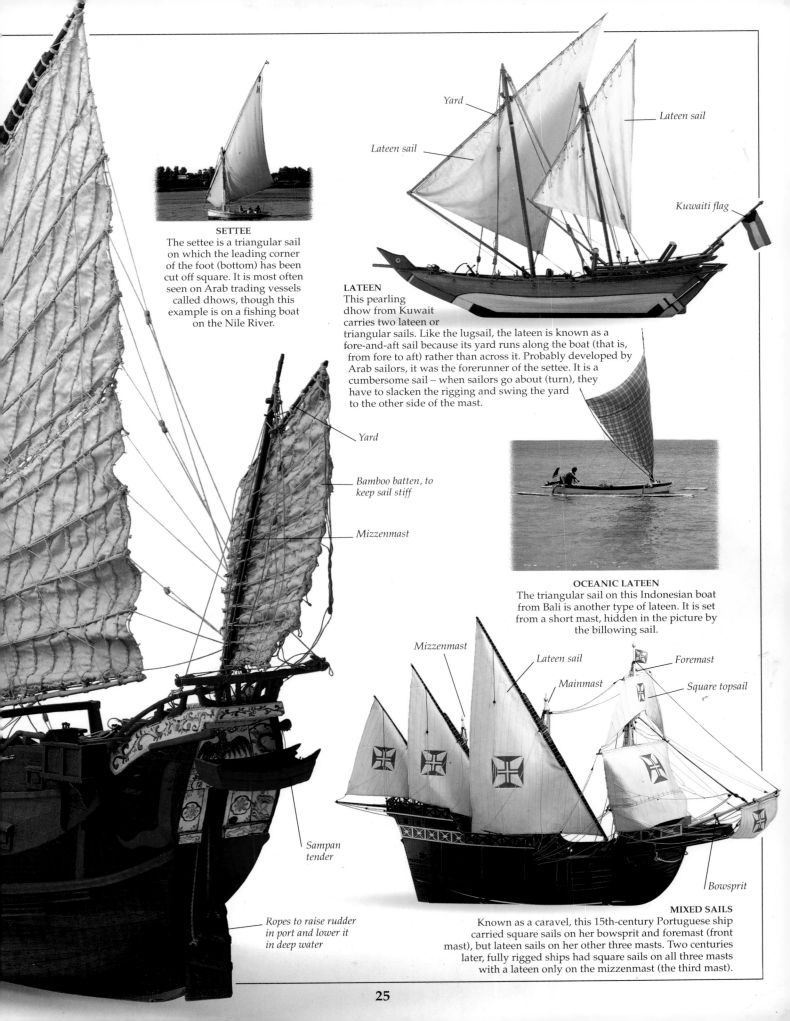

SETTEE
The settee is a triangular sail on which the leading corner of the foot (bottom) has been cut off square. It is most often seen on Arab trading vessels called dhows, though this example is on a fishing boat on the Nile River.

Yard

Lateen sail

Lateen sail

Kuwaiti flag

LATEEN
This pearling dhow from Kuwait carries two lateen or triangular sails. Like the lugsail, the lateen is known as a fore-and-aft sail because its yard runs along the boat (that is, from fore to aft) rather than across it. Probably developed by Arab sailors, it was the forerunner of the settee. It is a cumbersome sail – when sailors go about (turn), they have to slacken the rigging and swing the yard to the other side of the mast.

Yard

Bamboo batten, to keep sail stiff

Mizzenmast

OCEANIC LATEEN
The triangular sail on this Indonesian boat from Bali is another type of lateen. It is set from a short mast, hidden in the picture by the billowing sail.

Mizzenmast

Lateen sail

Mainmast

Foremast

Square topsail

Sampan tender

Bowsprit

Ropes to raise rudder in port and lower it in deep water

MIXED SAILS
Known as a caravel, this 15th-century Portuguese ship carried square sails on her bowsprit and foremast (front mast), but lateen sails on her other three masts. Two centuries later, fully rigged ships had square sails on all three masts with a lateen only on the mizzenmast (the third mast).

The Age of Sail

LIKE SPACESHIPS, SAILING SHIPS traveled to new worlds. In the 15th century, they took Christopher Columbus to America and Vasco da Gama around Africa to India. Three hundred years later a sailing ship took James Cook to the South Seas and on to Australia. Thanks to the sailing ship, the continents and oceans were explored and charted. In the wake of the explorers came trading ships carrying exotic spices, textiles, tobacco, and other products of the Orient and the Americas to Europe. Over the centuries, sailing the seven seas was a way of life for many men (and the occasional woman). There were always decks to caulk, yards to brace, watches to keep, and sails to reef, furl, and mend. And ever present was the sea, always unpredictable and capable of rising in the sudden fury of a storm.

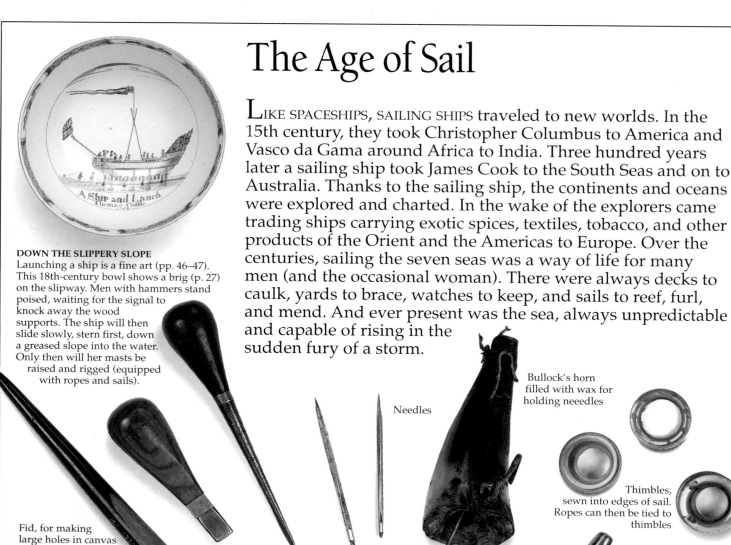

DOWN THE SLIPPERY SLOPE
Launching a ship is a fine art (pp. 46–47). This 18th-century bowl shows a brig (p. 27) on the slipway. Men with hammers stand poised, waiting for the signal to knock away the wood supports. The ship will then slide slowly, stern first, down a greased slope into the water. Only then will her masts be raised and rigged (equipped with ropes and sails).

Fid, for making large holes in canvas

Seam rubber

Needles

Pricker, for making small holes in canvas

Bullock's horn filled with wax for holding neeedles

Thimbles, sewn into edges of sail. Ropes can then be tied to thimbles

Hole for thumb

Punch set for making thimbles

Sailmaker's palm

Twine

TOOLS OF THE SAILMAKER
Until recently, sails were made by hand by sewing strips of heavy canvas together. Every large ship had a sailmaker in its crew, as sails were often damaged and had to be mended at sea. The sailmaker's tools included a "rubber," used to make sharp creases in the canvas before sewing, and a palm, to protect the hand from the needle as it pushed the needle through the canvas.

IN THE SAILMAKER'S LOFT
This sailmaker is finishing a seam, while another sail is being stretched. Both sails will be finished by sewing a rope all the way around their edges.

Foremast

Mainmast

Fore royal

Main royal

Fore topgallant

Main topgallant
studding sails

POOPED
Caught in a storm, this ship
(the *Joseph Sampson*) is in danger
of being pooped. Pooping happens
when a wave breaks over the
stern. This may cause the ship
to veer wildly off course. If
she turns across the waves,
she may capsize.

Fore topsail

Flying jib

Outer jib

Inner jib

Bowsprit

Gaff sail

Dolphin striker, for
holding down bowsprit

Lower
studding sail

Boom for
studding sail

Figurehead

Fore staysail

Foresail

FULL SAIL AHEAD
This is a merchant ship of the mid-19th century.
Because she has two masts, both rigged with square sails, she is
technically known as a brig. She is sailing with a light wind behind
her, and her crew has set as many sails as they can. From the ends
of the main, top, and topgallant yards, short yards and booms
have been run out to set extra sails. These "studding sails" were
carried by all sailing ships from early in the 18th century.

KEEPING THE WATER OUT
The caulker keeps a ship's
planks watertight, by driving
old rope into the seams
between them and then
sealing them with tar.

SHIPWORM
Shipworms like
the teredo bore
holes into the wood hulls
of sailing ships. By the late
17th century, many ships were
sheathed with copper plates
to keep the destructive
mollusks out.

SEA GROWTH
This bottle was
pulled from the
sea encrusted with
barnacles. These
sticky crustaceans also
attach themselves to the
hulls of wood ships,
slowing the vessels down.

27

Continued on next page

Sailing for a living

In ships laden with tea from China, manufactured goods from Europe, and sugar from the West Indies, sailors spent many months away from home. They had to be tough. They lived in cramped and filthy conditions and their diet was poor – after the first few days at sea there would be no more fresh vegetables or fruit. For all this, sailors were poorly paid. A few became pirates, making a more profitable living by stealing the cargoes of other ships.

SAILOR'S FAREWELL
The sailor saying goodbye to his sweetheart was a popular theme for 18th-century artists.

SHOW A LEG
The hammock was adopted from the natives of the West Indies in the 16th century. Before then, sailors slept on the deck.

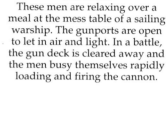

OFF DUTY
These men are relaxing over a meal at the mess table of a sailing warship. The gunports are open to let in air and light. In a battle, the gun deck is cleared away and the men busy themselves rapidly loading and firing the cannon.

HARDTACK
Sailors in the British navy were issued with 1 lb ($\frac{1}{2}$ kg) of these rock-hard biscuits every day.

SUGAR ISLAND
This 17th-century map of Barbados shows a sugar mill worked by slaves. Sugar plantations in the West Indies made vast fortunes for their owners.

PREVENTATIVE MEDICINE
To keep from getting the disease scurvy, which is caused by a lack of vitamin C, British sailors ate limes. This made American sailors nickname them "Limeys."

FELLOW TRAVELER
The holds of most ships were infested with rats. Fleas that lived on the rats carried the plague from country to country.

BARBADOS WATERS
These measuring jugs and 6 gallon (27-liter) breaker (water cask) are for issuing daily rations of "Barbados waters" – rum – to British sailors. Rum is distilled from sugar cane and was favored on board ship because it kept much longer than beer. Lower-ranked sailors were given grog, a mixture of four parts water to one part rum.

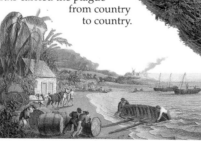

ROLL OUT THE BARREL
On the West Indian island of Antigua, barrels of sugar are loaded onto a boat that will then carry them to the trading ship anchored offshore. In a few weeks, the sugar will be for sale in Europe.

PORT OF CALL
This picture is of Portsmouth, England, early in the 19th century. Like all ports, it had a lively and sometimes violent neighborhood where sailors could enjoy themselves and spend their pay.

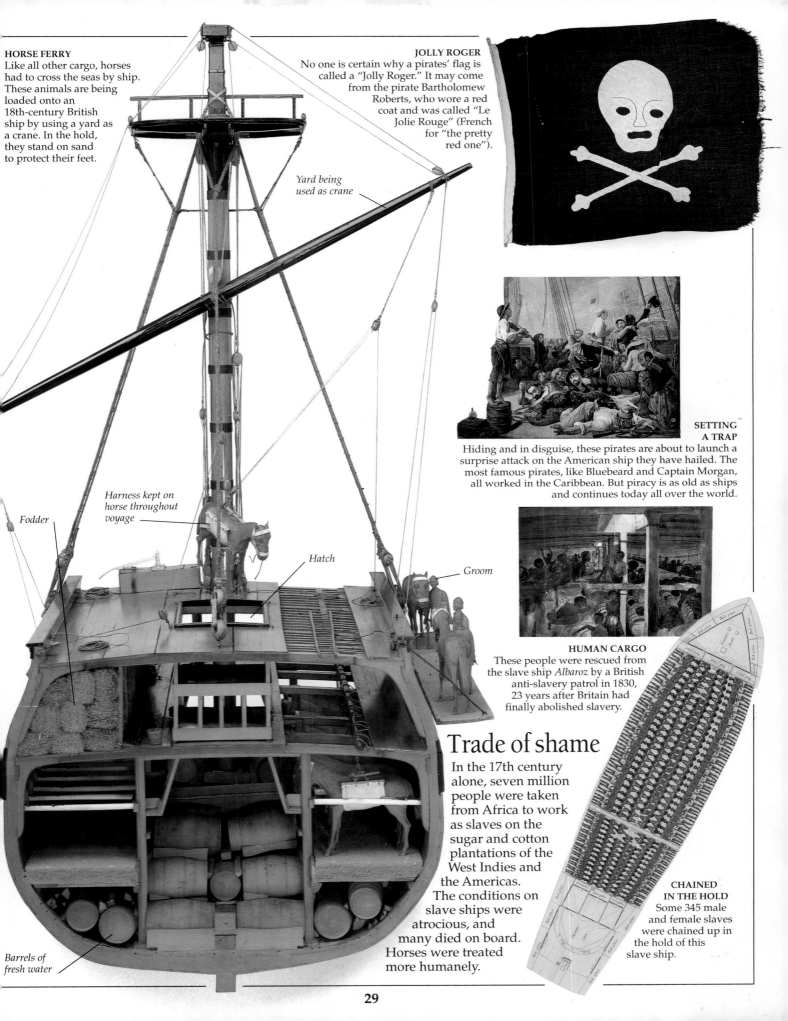

HORSE FERRY

Like all other cargo, horses had to cross the seas by ship. These animals are being loaded onto an 18th-century British ship by using a yard as a crane. In the hold, they stand on sand to protect their feet.

JOLLY ROGER

No one is certain why a pirates' flag is called a "Jolly Roger." It may come from the pirate Bartholomew Roberts, who wore a red coat and was called "Le Jolie Rouge" (French for "the pretty red one").

Yard being used as crane

Fodder

Harness kept on horse throughout voyage

Hatch

Groom

SETTING A TRAP

Hiding and in disguise, these pirates are about to launch a surprise attack on the American ship they have hailed. The most famous pirates, like Bluebeard and Captain Morgan, all worked in the Caribbean. But piracy is as old as ships and continues today all over the world.

HUMAN CARGO

These people were rescued from the slave ship *Albaroz* by a British anti-slavery patrol in 1830, 23 years after Britain had finally abolished slavery.

Trade of shame

In the 17th century alone, seven million people were taken from Africa to work as slaves on the sugar and cotton plantations of the West Indies and the Americas. The conditions on slave ships were atrocious, and many died on board. Horses were treated more humanely.

CHAINED IN THE HOLD

Some 345 male and female slaves were chained up in the hold of this slave ship.

Barrels of fresh water

Thar' she blows!

Slot through which harpoon line runs

W HEN HE SPIED a column of water vapor rising from the sea, the lookout on board a whaling ship raised the alarm with the traditional cry of "Thar' she blows!" Small boats were launched and rowed out to harpoon the whale, which had given away its presence by coming to the surface and breathing. For hundreds of years, local hunters all over the world have launched boats from the beach to chase whales for meat. But in the heyday of whaling in the early 19th century, American and European whalers (whaling ships) undertook long voyages around the world in pursuit of these ocean giants. The cruel and bloody hunt kept the world light and clean, for whale oil was burned in lamps and used to make soap and cosmetics. With the discovery of a more abundant oil – petroleum – in the 1860s, the demand for whales declined. But despite strong protests, whaling for meat continues in several countries to this day.

Sail of matted palm leaves

Harpoon

Paddle

INDONESIAN WHALER
The people of Lamalera on the Indonesian island of Lembata hunt sperm whales from boats like this. Like 19th-century European whale hunters, they use hand-thrown harpoons to catch the whales, which are often two to three times longer than the boats that hunt them.

WOODEN WHALE
Carved by a sailor on a long voyage, this wooden model of a sperm whale is inlaid with a harpoon of bone. The sperm whale's huge square head is full of a liquid wax called spermaceti, which was used to make candles and cosmetics. The right whale and the sperm whale were the most commercially valued. But all ten species of great whale (including the largest animal ever to have lived, the blue whale) have been hunted, some almost to the point of extinction.

TOOLS OF THE TRADE
The boat hook is a general tool used to bring anything – be it a rope or a whale – toward the boat. These sharp harpoons, hurled into the surfacing whale, have pivoting barbs on their heads to keep them firmly lodged in the animal's flesh. The lance was not thrown but stabbed into the whale. The broad boat spade was used to cut out a hole in the whale's tail through which a towing rope could then be tied.

Harpoon

Spare harpoon

Boat hook

Lance

Line

Boat spade

HARPOONING
The whale would dive when struck by the harpoon, which was tied to a very long line of rope. The whaleboat would be towed through the water until the whale surfaced to breathe and then dived again. This could go on for hours. When the exhausted animal surfaced for the last time, the boat would close in and the bowman would kill it by driving a lance into its underbelly.

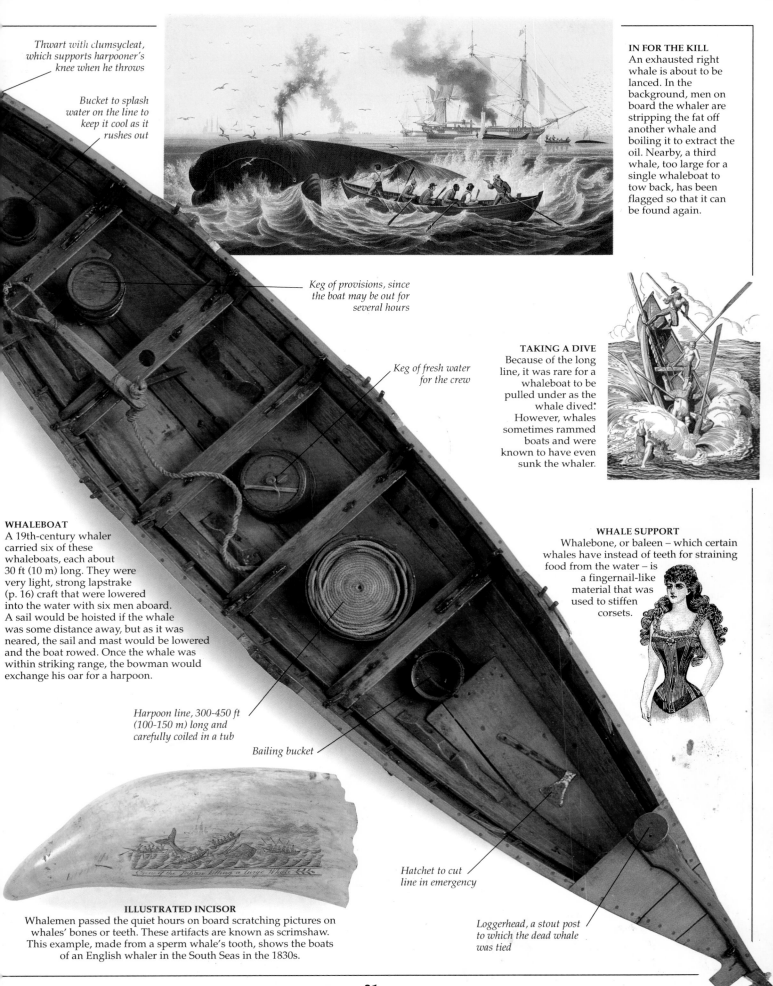

Thwart with clumsycleat, which supports harpooner's knee when he throws

Bucket to splash water on the line to keep it cool as it rushes out

IN FOR THE KILL
An exhausted right whale is about to be lanced. In the background, men on board the whaler are stripping the fat off another whale and boiling it to extract the oil. Nearby, a third whale, too large for a single whaleboat to tow back, has been flagged so that it can be found again.

Keg of provisions, since the boat may be out for several hours

Keg of fresh water for the crew

TAKING A DIVE
Because of the long line, it was rare for a whaleboat to be pulled under as the whale dived. However, whales sometimes rammed boats and were known to have even sunk the whaler.

WHALEBOAT
A 19th-century whaler carried six of these whaleboats, each about 30 ft (10 m) long. They were very light, strong lapstrake (p. 16) craft that were lowered into the water with six men aboard. A sail would be hoisted if the whale was some distance away, but as it was neared, the sail and mast would be lowered and the boat rowed. Once the whale was within striking range, the bowman would exchange his oar for a harpoon.

WHALE SUPPORT
Whalebone, or baleen – which certain whales have instead of teeth for straining food from the water – is a fingernail-like material that was used to stiffen corsets.

Harpoon line, 300-450 ft (100-150 m) long and carefully coiled in a tub

Bailing bucket

ILLUSTRATED INCISOR
Whalemen passed the quiet hours on board scratching pictures on whales' bones or teeth. These artifacts are known as scrimshaw. This example, made from a sperm whale's tooth, shows the boats of an English whaler in the South Seas in the 1830s.

Hatchet to cut line in emergency

Loggerhead, a stout post to which the dead whale was tied

A splash of color

PERHAPS BECAUSE THEIR LIVES depend on them, people have strong affections for their boats. To make them more beautiful or individual, sailboats and ships are often decorated with paintwork or elaborate carvings. Traditionally sailing ships had a carved or painted figure – the figurehead – on the bow, which often reflected the ship's name. In contrast, modern motor and steam ships are hardly decorated at all.

Polished steel

Painted wood

VENETIAN STEEL
The steel bow of the gondola (p. 34) protects it and acts as a counterbalance to the weight of the gondolier at the stern. The six prongs symbolize the six districts into which Venice is divided.

ROMAN BIRD
Forged in the 1st century A.D., this bronze goose head probably adorned the stern of a small Roman merchant ship.

DOGFISH HEAD
A fanciful creature – half dog, half fish – decorates the bow of this 18th-century barge made for the British royal family.

Winged figure of victory

PRETTY PENNY
This coin shows the bow of a warship with an oculus (eye). It commemorates the Cypriot victory in the sea battle of Salamis in 306 B.C.

Notch where boom sits

Boom crutch for fishing boat from Surabaja, Indonesia

POLYNESIAN STYLE
A 15th-century Maori craftsman from the North Island of New Zealand carved this figure to adorn a canoe.

SALTY STERN
This colorful stern belongs to a very functional boat, a wooden *jangola* that carries salt between the Indonesian island of Madura and the mainland.

MYSTERIOUS PRESIDENT
This figurehead of Abraham Lincoln was washed up on a beach in the Scilly Isles off the southwest coast of England. What ship it came from, how it sank, and what happened to its crew are all mysteries.

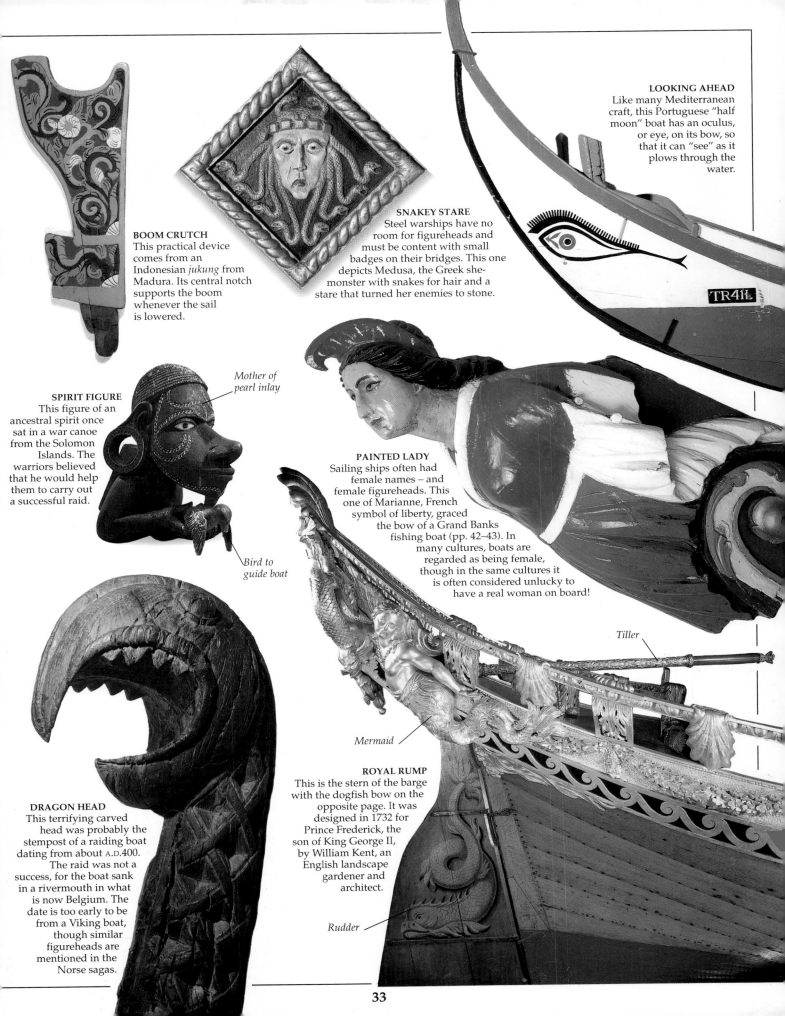

BOOM CRUTCH
This practical device comes from an Indonesian *jukung* from Madura. Its central notch supports the boom whenever the sail is lowered.

SNAKEY STARE
Steel warships have no room for figureheads and must be content with small badges on their bridges. This one depicts Medusa, the Greek she-monster with snakes for hair and a stare that turned her enemies to stone.

LOOKING AHEAD
Like many Mediterranean craft, this Portuguese "half moon" boat has an oculus, or eye, on its bow, so that it can "see" as it plows through the water.

Mother of pearl inlay

SPIRIT FIGURE
This figure of an ancestral spirit once sat in a war canoe from the Solomon Islands. The warriors believed that he would help them to carry out a successful raid.

Bird to guide boat

PAINTED LADY
Sailing ships often had female names – and female figureheads. This one of Marianne, French symbol of liberty, graced the bow of a Grand Banks fishing boat (pp. 42–43). In many cultures, boats are regarded as being female, though in the same cultures it is often considered unlucky to have a real woman on board!

Tiller

Mermaid

DRAGON HEAD
This terrifying carved head was probably the stempost of a raiding boat dating from about A.D.400. The raid was not a success, for the boat sank in a rivermouth in what is now Belgium. The date is too early to be from a Viking boat, though similar figureheads are mentioned in the Norse sagas.

ROYAL RUMP
This is the stern of the barge with the dogfish bow on the opposite page. It was designed in 1732 for Prince Frederick, the son of King George II, by William Kent, an English landscape gardener and architect.

Rudder

In sheltered waters

Skewed stern

TRANSPORTING PEOPLE AND GOODS on water has always been cheaper than transporting them on land. Most countries have rivers, lakes, lagoons, and other natural waterways. Many nations have added to these by building extensive canal systems along which cargo barges sail, steam, punt, or are towed. Great canals like the ones at Suez and Panama were dug to shorten the journeys of ocean-going ships. Special boats have been developed on all these inland waterways. Some are built to be highly maneuverable for work in confined spaces, like the asymmetrical gondola which ferries passengers along the narrow canals of Venice. Most are flat-bottomed, so they can run aground without getting stuck or tipping over. A flat bottom also gives a boat more cargo space, but the absence of a keel makes it hard to handle in rough waters. So some canal boats have leeboards, strong side-mounted stabilizers that make them more seaworthy.

CROOKED CONSTRUCTION
The gondola is fatter and wider on one side, the port side, than the other. This means the gondolier can row with one oar and still go in a straight line.

VENETIAN WATER TAXI
This gondola is ready for a wedding party. Rich families used to compete to have the most lavish gondolas, until the Venetian state decreed that they must all be black (p. 32).

HONG KONG HOUSEBOATS
On the incredibly crowded island of Hong Kong, many people make their homes on small, flat-bottomed boats called junks (pp. 24–25) or sampans.

GREEK SHIPPING LANE
Saltwater canals, like this one which was built between the Gulf of Corinth and the Saronic Gulf, are examples of making the water suit the ships, rather than making the ships suit the water!

ONE-HORSE POWER
Towpaths were laid alongside the canals built in Britain in the 18th and into the 19th centuries, so that the narrow barges could be towed by horses.

FRESH FISH FERRY
A Chinese merchant uses this sampan, Chinese for "three planks," to collect fish from fishermen all around Lake Donting. He loads the live fish into compartments in the hull and takes them to a market down the Yangtze River. The countless miles of rivers, lakes, and canals that cross China have given rise to hundreds of types of sampan.

Support for rain canopy

Sliding awning

Bamboo punt pole for pushing boat along

Open stern where two outboard motors are mounted

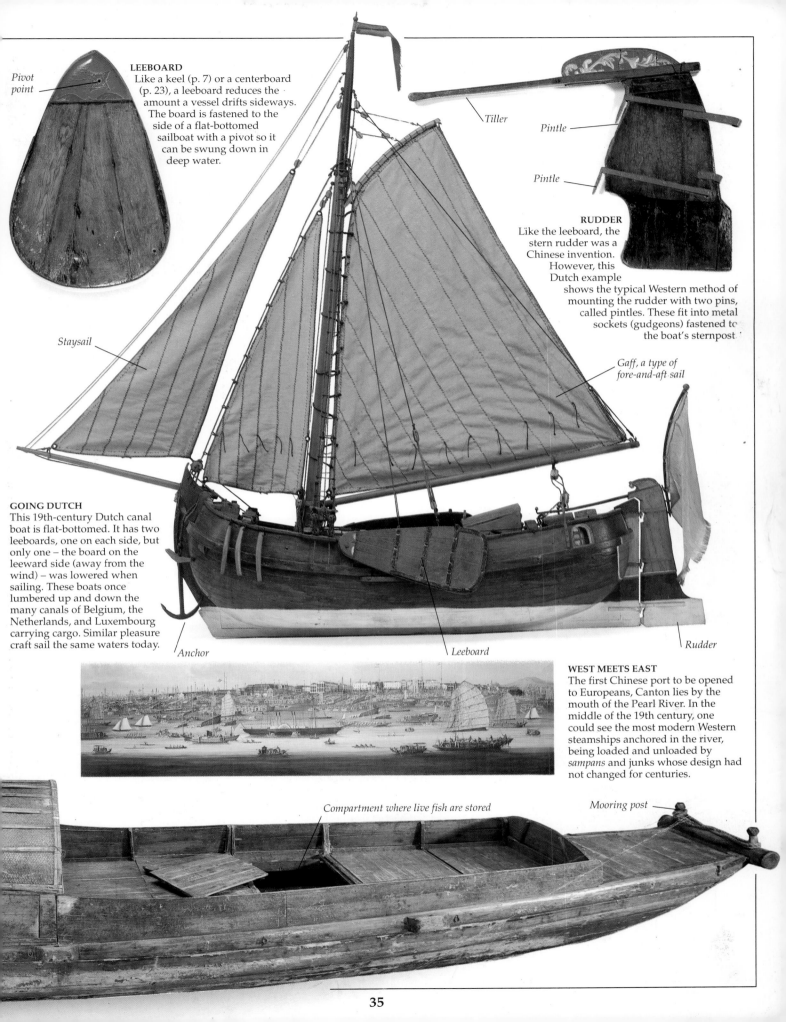

LEEBOARD
Like a keel (p. 7) or a centerboard (p. 23), a leeboard reduces the amount a vessel drifts sideways. The board is fastened to the side of a flat-bottomed sailboat with a pivot so it can be swung down in deep water.

Pivot point

Tiller

Pintle

Pintle

RUDDER
Like the leeboard, the stern rudder was a Chinese invention. However, this Dutch example shows the typical Western method of mounting the rudder with two pins, called pintles. These fit into metal sockets (gudgeons) fastened to the boat's sternpost.

Staysail

Gaff, a type of fore-and-aft sail

GOING DUTCH
This 19th-century Dutch canal boat is flat-bottomed. It has two leeboards, one on each side, but only one – the board on the leeward side (away from the wind) – was lowered when sailing. These boats once lumbered up and down the many canals of Belgium, the Netherlands, and Luxembourg carrying cargo. Similar pleasure craft sail the same waters today.

Anchor

Leeboard

Rudder

WEST MEETS EAST
The first Chinese port to be opened to Europeans, Canton lies by the mouth of the Pearl River. In the middle of the 19th century, one could see the most modern Western steamships anchored in the river, being loaded and unloaded by *sampans* and junks whose design had not changed for centuries.

Compartment where live fish are stored

Mooring post

Steam and paddle wheels

As THE STEAM ENGINE was developed in the 18th century, inventors and engineers experimented with new mechanical ways of driving boats and ships. The first big development was the paddle wheel. As one of these huge wheels turned, its flat blades dipped into the water and pushed a vessel along. Paddle wheelers were very maneuverable and were soon traveling all around the world. But they were particularly suited to the shallow waters of rivers and lakes. The most famous were the elegant paddle wheelers of the Mississippi, some of which are still going strong – the world's largest riverboat is the *Mississippi Queen*. However, for sea-going ships the propeller soon gained the upper hand.

UP A CREEK
Paddle wheelers are too wide for narrow rivers. In *The African Queen*, movie stars Humphrey Bogart and Katherine Hepburn had enough trouble navigating a small screw steamer in the rivers of East Africa.

PALATIAL FREIGHTERS
In their day, the Mississippi paddle wheelers were as luxurious as the great sea-going liners of a later age (pp. 54–57). But first and foremost they were cargo carriers, collecting produce and delivering supplies to some 50 stops on the river between Memphis and New Orleans.

STERN-WHEELER
Instead of two paddle wheels, one on each side, stern-wheelers have a single wheel at the rear. They can work in shallower water than side-wheelers. This is a modern replica of the stern-wheeler *Natchez*. In her first year, 1894, she made 50 trips between New Orleans and Vickersburg and carried over 56,000 bales of cotton.

STEAMER NATCHEZ
PORT OF NEW ORLEANS

Entrance to below-deck accommodations

"Sponson," or paddle cover

CATCH A PACKET
The *King Alfred* was a packet steamer, a boat that carried passengers and freight on short, fixed routes.

Sponson

PUBLIC TRANSPORTATION, 1905
The *King Alfred* was one of 30 paddle wheelers commissioned by London's council to ease the pressure on the city's busy roads and railways. But the service was not popular and was stopped two years after it began. The *King Alfred* went on to Germany, where she made excursion trips on the Rhine and Elbe rivers until she was broken up (scrapped) in 1965.

STEAMING ACROSS THE ATLANTIC
In 1819, *Savannah* became the first steamer to cross the Atlantic, taking 21 days to travel from her home port in Georgia to Liverpool. However, she relied on her sails for most of the voyage. It was another 19 years before *Sirius*, a British ship, made the first crossing entirely under steam.

RECORD BREAKER
A cross-section of *Persia* shows her huge paddle wheels, each 40 ft (12 m) in diameter. She was built in 1860 to be the fastest ship across the Atlantic and went on to make several record-breaking runs.

Crankshaft

Paddle blade

Benches on deck

STEAMING UP
This is a 320-horsepower marine beam engine from the 1840s. A coal fire heats fresh water to generate steam. The steam travels along pipes to the cylinder, where it forces a piston to move. The piston moves the beam and crankshaft, which then turns the paddle wheel.

Cylinder casing

Steam outlet

Piston rod

BEST OF BOTH WHIRLS
Launched in 1858, the *Great Eastern* (p. 47) was six times bigger than any ship yet made. She had both paddle wheels for shallow water and a screw propeller for speed in the open ocean.

Turn of the screw

IN 1845 A TUG-OF-WAR was held between a paddle wheeler and a steamer powered by a propeller, or "screw." The propeller proved to be the stronger of the two, pulling the paddle wheeler backward through the water. By that date many people were working on perfecting the propeller, including John Ericsson and Francis Pettit Smith. Even then the idea was a very old one. The ancient Greeks raised water with the help of Archimedes' screw, a device that looks like a corkscrew in a tube. As the screw turns, its thread pulls water up the tube. Some early propellers were a shortened version of the same device. Others were made by setting several angled blades around a central hub (boss). Modern propellers are similarly shaped, and all but the biggest have two, three, or four blades. They are still often called screws.

YOUNG BLADE
The Swedish inventor John Ericsson developed a propeller shaped like a corkscrew. After some experiments in England, his idea was successfully applied to American river steamers.

EARLY PUSHER
This propeller is a "common screw," the most successful type of propeller up until 1860. Only then did engineers find that rounded blade tips were more efficient because they caused less vibration.

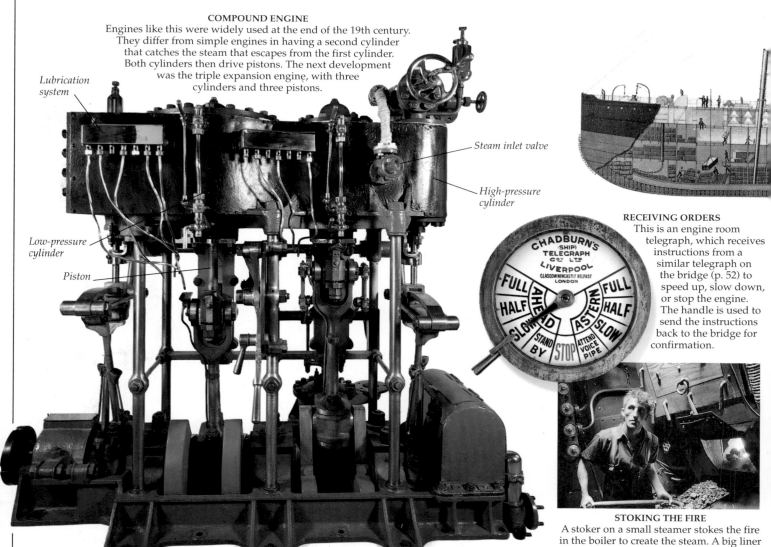

COMPOUND ENGINE
Engines like this were widely used at the end of the 19th century. They differ from simple engines in having a second cylinder that catches the steam that escapes from the first cylinder. Both cylinders then drive pistons. The next development was the triple expansion engine, with three cylinders and three pistons.

Lubrication system

Low-pressure cylinder

Piston

Steam inlet valve

High-pressure cylinder

RECEIVING ORDERS
This is an engine room telegraph, which receives instructions from a similar telegraph on the bridge (p. 52) to speed up, slow down, or stop the engine. The handle is used to send the instructions back to the bridge for confirmation.

CHADBURN'S (SHIP) TELEGRAPH Cʸ Lᵀᴰ LIVERPOOL GLASGOW NEWCASTLE BELFAST LONDON
FULL AHEAD HALF SLOW STAND BY STOP ATTEND VOICE PIPE FULL ASTERN HALF SLOW

STOKING THE FIRE
A stoker on a small steamer stokes the fire in the boiler to create the steam. A big liner had more than 180 stokers, each feeding 5 tons of coal into the furnaces every day.

FIT FOR A QUEEN
Each of the *Queen Mary's* (p. 55) four propellers was 18 ft (5.5 m) in diameter and weighed 38.5 tons. Cast in London, the monster screws were then taken to a shipyard on the Clyde River for fitting.

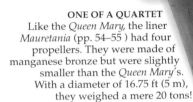

BLADE EDGES
The blades of a propeller (in this case a common screw) are helices – like sections of a spiral.

ONE OF A QUARTET
Like the *Queen Mary*, the liner *Mauretania* (pp. 54–55) had four propellers. They were made of manganese bronze but were slightly smaller than the *Queen Mary's*. With a diameter of 16.75 ft (5 m), they weighed a mere 20 tons!

TURN OF SPEED
The *Mauretania's* propellers could turn 180 times a minute. Four-bladed propellers are the most common for large ships, but two- and three-bladed ones are also made. Supertanker screws (p. 50) often have five blades.

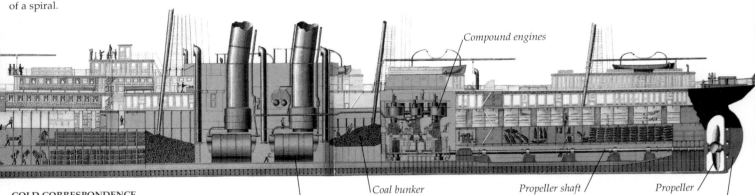

Compound engines

Coal bunker

Propeller shaft

Propeller

Rudder

Boiler, which heats water to form steam

COLD CORRESPONDENCE
Built in 1879 for the British-Australian mail run, the *Orient* was the first steamer to carry refrigerated cargo. She was a single-screw ship powered by a compound engine. On her trial she averaged over 18 mph (29 km/h).

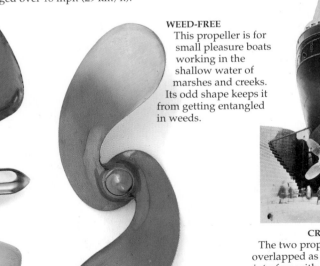

WEED-FREE
This propeller is for small pleasure boats working in the shallow water of marshes and creeks. Its odd shape keeps it from getting entangled in weeds.

CROSSED BLADES
The two propellers on the liner *Teutonic* overlapped as they spun. But they did not interfere with each other because the port screw was positioned 6 ft (1.8 m) in front of the starboard one.

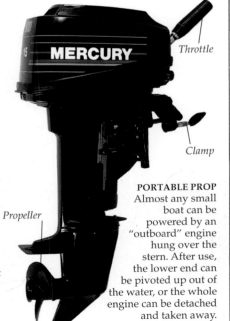

MERCURY

Throttle

Clamp

Propeller

PORTABLE PROP
Almost any small boat can be powered by an "outboard" engine hung over the stern. After use, the lower end can be pivoted up out of the water, or the whole engine can be detached and taken away.

Last days of the merchant sail

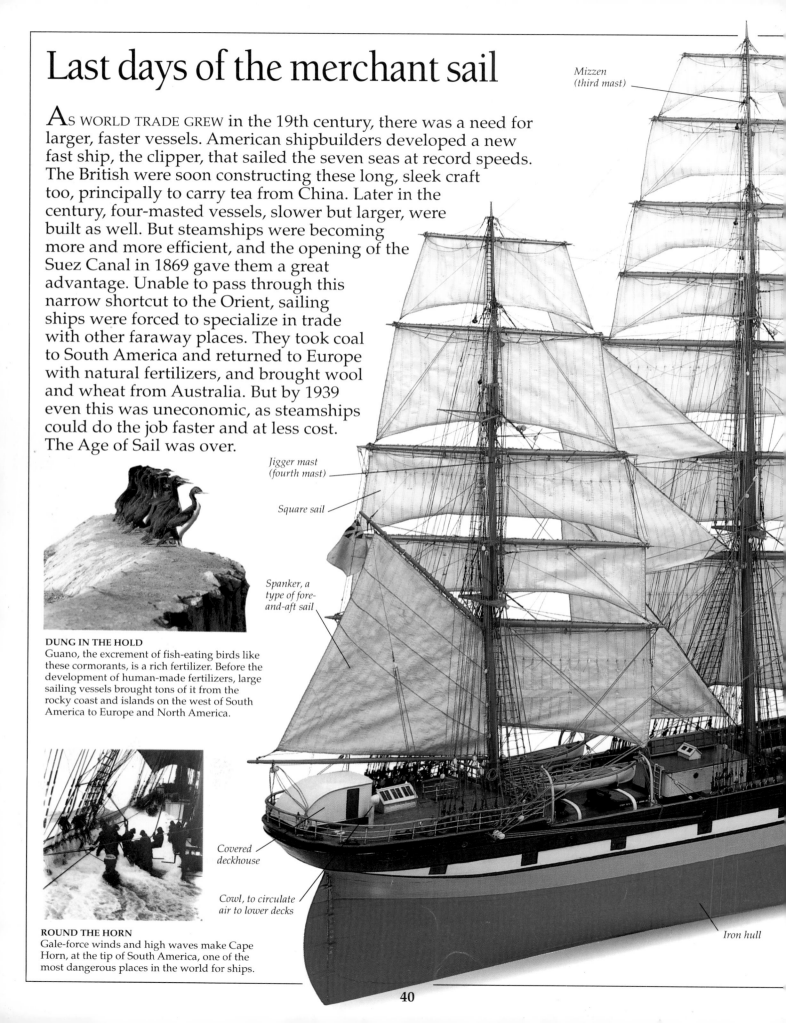

AS WORLD TRADE GREW in the 19th century, there was a need for larger, faster vessels. American shipbuilders developed a new fast ship, the clipper, that sailed the seven seas at record speeds. The British were soon constructing these long, sleek craft too, principally to carry tea from China. Later in the century, four-masted vessels, slower but larger, were built as well. But steamships were becoming more and more efficient, and the opening of the Suez Canal in 1869 gave them a great advantage. Unable to pass through this narrow shortcut to the Orient, sailing ships were forced to specialize in trade with other faraway places. They took coal to South America and returned to Europe with natural fertilizers, and brought wool and wheat from Australia. But by 1939 even this was uneconomic, as steamships could do the job faster and at less cost. The Age of Sail was over.

Mizzen (third mast)

Jigger mast (fourth mast)

Square sail

Spanker, a type of fore-and-aft sail

Covered deckhouse

Cowl, to circulate air to lower decks

Iron hull

DUNG IN THE HOLD
Guano, the excrement of fish-eating birds like these cormorants, is a rich fertilizer. Before the development of human-made fertilizers, large sailing vessels brought tons of it from the rocky coast and islands on the west of South America to Europe and North America.

ROUND THE HORN
Gale-force winds and high waves make Cape Horn, at the tip of South America, one of the most dangerous places in the world for ships.

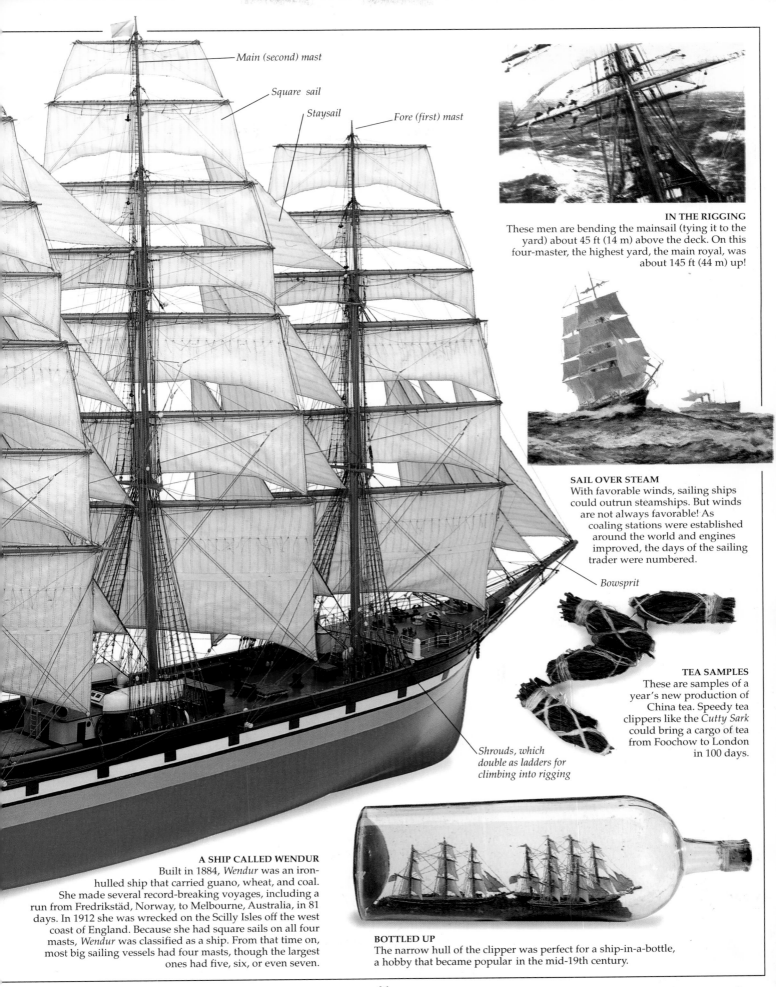

Main (second) mast

Square sail

Staysail

Fore (first) mast

IN THE RIGGING
These men are bending the mainsail (tying it to the yard) about 45 ft (14 m) above the deck. On this four-master, the highest yard, the main royal, was about 145 ft (44 m) up!

SAIL OVER STEAM
With favorable winds, sailing ships could outrun steamships. But winds are not always favorable! As coaling stations were established around the world and engines improved, the days of the sailing trader were numbered.

Bowsprit

TEA SAMPLES
These are samples of a year's new production of China tea. Speedy tea clippers like the *Cutty Sark* could bring a cargo of tea from Foochow to London in 100 days.

Shrouds, which double as ladders for climbing into rigging

A SHIP CALLED WENDUR
Built in 1884, *Wendur* was an iron-hulled ship that carried guano, wheat, and coal. She made several record-breaking voyages, including a run from Fredrikstäd, Norway, to Melbourne, Australia, in 81 days. In 1912 she was wrecked on the Scilly Isles off the west coast of England. Because she had square sails on all four masts, *Wendur* was classified as a ship. From that time on, most big sailing vessels had four masts, though the largest ones had five, six, or even seven.

BOTTLED UP
The narrow hull of the clipper was perfect for a ship-in-a-bottle, a hobby that became popular in the mid-19th century.

Hook, line, and sinker

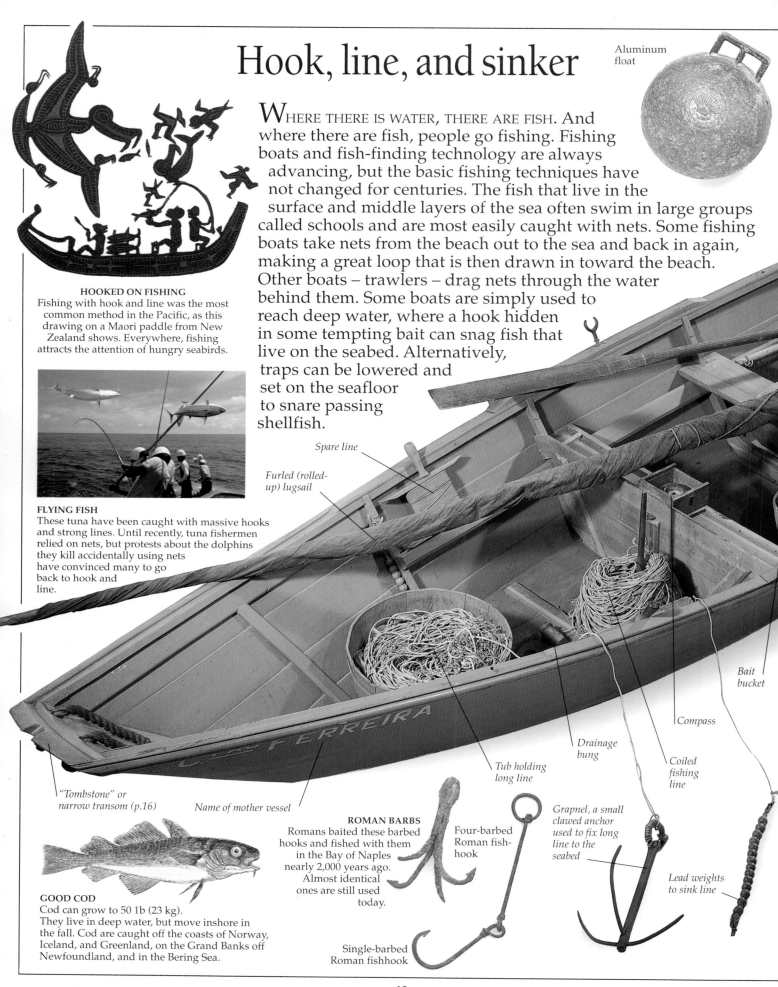

Aluminum float

WHERE THERE IS WATER, THERE ARE FISH. And where there are fish, people go fishing. Fishing boats and fish-finding technology are always advancing, but the basic fishing techniques have not changed for centuries. The fish that live in the surface and middle layers of the sea often swim in large groups called schools and are most easily caught with nets. Some fishing boats take nets from the beach out to the sea and back in again, making a great loop that is then drawn in toward the beach. Other boats – trawlers – drag nets through the water behind them. Some boats are simply used to reach deep water, where a hook hidden in some tempting bait can snag fish that live on the seabed. Alternatively, traps can be lowered and set on the seafloor to snare passing shellfish.

HOOKED ON FISHING
Fishing with hook and line was the most common method in the Pacific, as this drawing on a Maori paddle from New Zealand shows. Everywhere, fishing attracts the attention of hungry seabirds.

FLYING FISH
These tuna have been caught with massive hooks and strong lines. Until recently, tuna fishermen relied on nets, but protests about the dolphins they kill accidentally using nets have convinced many to go back to hook and line.

Spare line

Furled (rolled-up) lugsail

Bait bucket

Compass

Drainage bung

Coiled fishing line

Tub holding long line

"Tombstone" or narrow transom (p.16)

Name of mother vessel

ROMAN BARBS
Romans baited these barbed hooks and fished with them in the Bay of Naples nearly 2,000 years ago. Almost identical ones are still used today.

Four-barbed Roman fish-hook

Grapnel, a small clawed anchor used to fix long line to the seabed

Lead weights to sink line

Single-barbed Roman fishhook

GOOD COD
Cod can grow to 50 1b (23 kg). They live in deep water, but move inshore in the fall. Cod are caught off the coasts of Norway, Iceland, and Greenland, on the Grand Banks off Newfoundland, and in the Bering Sea.

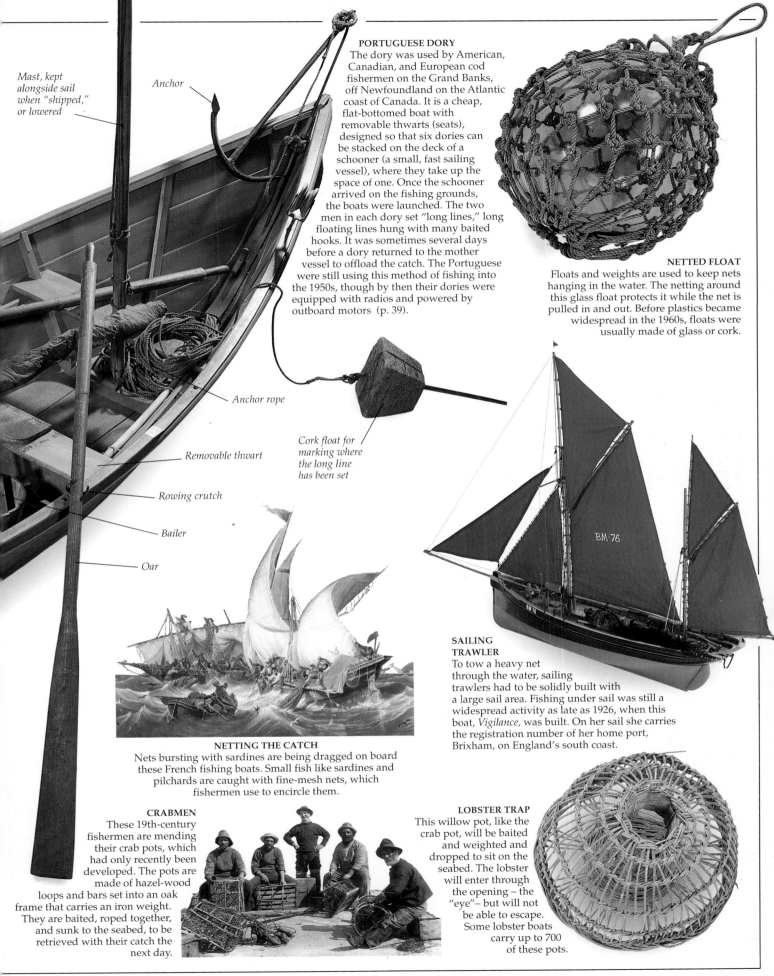

Mast, kept alongside sail when "shipped," or lowered

Anchor

PORTUGUESE DORY

The dory was used by American, Canadian, and European cod fishermen on the Grand Banks, off Newfoundland on the Atlantic coast of Canada. It is a cheap, flat-bottomed boat with removable thwarts (seats), designed so that six dories can be stacked on the deck of a schooner (a small, fast sailing vessel), where they take up the space of one. Once the schooner arrived on the fishing grounds, the boats were launched. The two men in each dory set "long lines," long floating lines hung with many baited hooks. It was sometimes several days before a dory returned to the mother vessel to offload the catch. The Portuguese were still using this method of fishing into the 1950s, though by then their dories were equipped with radios and powered by outboard motors (p. 39).

NETTED FLOAT

Floats and weights are used to keep nets hanging in the water. The netting around this glass float protects it while the net is pulled in and out. Before plastics became widespread in the 1960s, floats were usually made of glass or cork.

Anchor rope

Cork float for marking where the long line has been set

Removable thwart

Rowing crutch

Bailer

Oar

SAILING TRAWLER

To tow a heavy net through the water, sailing trawlers had to be solidly built with a large sail area. Fishing under sail was still a widespread activity as late as 1926, when this boat, *Vigilance*, was built. On her sail she carries the registration number of her home port, Brixham, on England's south coast.

NETTING THE CATCH

Nets bursting with sardines are being dragged on board these French fishing boats. Small fish like sardines and pilchards are caught with fine-mesh nets, which fishermen use to encircle them.

CRABMEN

These 19th-century fishermen are mending their crab pots, which had only recently been developed. The pots are made of hazel-wood loops and bars set into an oak frame that carries an iron weight. They are baited, roped together, and sunk to the seabed, to be retrieved with their catch the next day.

LOBSTER TRAP

This willow pot, like the crab pot, will be baited and weighted and dropped to sit on the seabed. The lobster will enter through the opening – the "eye"– but will not be able to escape. Some lobster boats carry up to 700 of these pots.

Continued on next page

Tangling and scooping

Nets come in a multitude of materials and sizes. The people of New Guinea once fished with hand-held scoops made of strong spiders' webs, modern commercial trawlers drag synthetic-fiber nets many miles long. But all nets work in one of two ways. Some have fairly big holes, so that fish trying to swim through them become entangled in the net. The most common of these are called gill nets, because they catch fish by the gills. Other nets are finer, and simply scoop up whole schools of fish. Some, like the whitebait net, are fixed in place and rely on the fish swimming into them. Others, like seine (encircling) and trawling nets, are dragged through the sea after the schools.

IN THE BAG
Full of fish, this is the "cod end" of a trawling net. It is a detachable bag to which long wings of netting are attached. Dragged through the water by ropes tied to these wings, the net is like a giant funnel.

A STERN VIEW
This German trawler, *Österreich*, has one large net that is hauled out of the water by winches mounted on the stern. Such "stern trawling" is a very common and productive fishing method in Northern Europe. Catches of 80 tons of herring in 20 minutes are not unusual.

STOWBOATERS
These river fishermen are catching small fish called whitebait with a stow net. Like a trawl net, it is funnel shaped. But instead of being dragged through the water, it is anchored to the riverbed to trap fish as they swim by.

Radio antenna

This is a red herring

Foremast derrick (crane)

Compass

Wheelhouse

Deck lights for night fishing

Trawl winch

Windlass for raising and lowering anchor

Hanging blocks for trawl net ropes

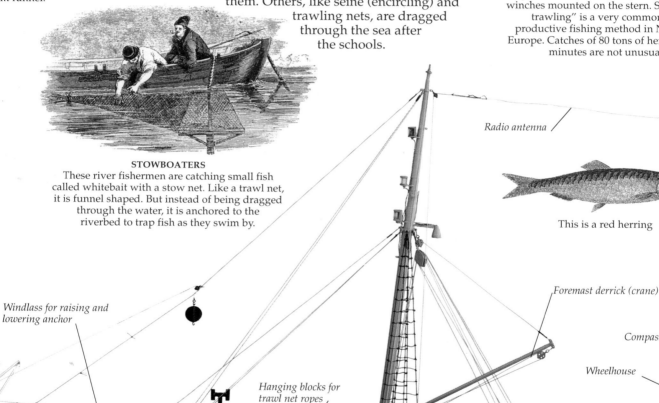

JOHN HENRY GY.000

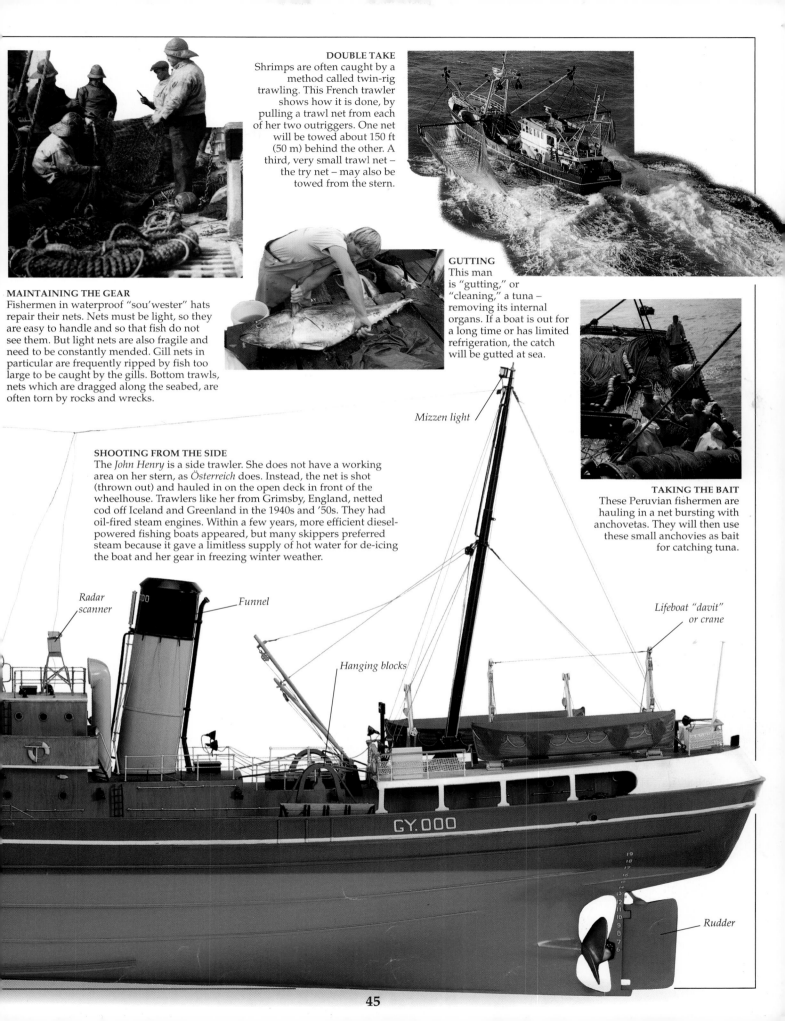

DOUBLE TAKE
Shrimps are often caught by a method called twin-rig trawling. This French trawler shows how it is done, by pulling a trawl net from each of her two outriggers. One net will be towed about 150 ft (50 m) behind the other. A third, very small trawl net – the try net – may also be towed from the stern.

GUTTING
This man is "gutting," or "cleaning," a tuna – removing its internal organs. If a boat is out for a long time or has limited refrigeration, the catch will be gutted at sea.

MAINTAINING THE GEAR
Fishermen in waterproof "sou'wester" hats repair their nets. Nets must be light, so they are easy to handle and so that fish do not see them. But light nets are also fragile and need to be constantly mended. Gill nets in particular are frequently ripped by fish too large to be caught by the gills. Bottom trawls, nets which are dragged along the seabed, are often torn by rocks and wrecks.

SHOOTING FROM THE SIDE
The *John Henry* is a side trawler. She does not have a working area on her stern, as *Österreich* does. Instead, the net is shot (thrown out) and hauled in on the open deck in front of the wheelhouse. Trawlers like her from Grimsby, England, netted cod off Iceland and Greenland in the 1940s and '50s. They had oil-fired steam engines. Within a few years, more efficient diesel-powered fishing boats appeared, but many skippers preferred steam because it gave a limitless supply of hot water for de-icing the boat and her gear in freezing winter weather.

Mizzen light

TAKING THE BAIT
These Peruvian fishermen are hauling in a net bursting with anchovetas. They will then use these small anchovies as bait for catching tuna.

Radar scanner

Funnel

Hanging blocks

Lifeboat "davit" or crane

GY.000

Rudder

Building in iron and steel

BREAK OUT
THE BUBBLY
When a ship is
launched, she is
christened with a
bottle of champagne
smashed over
her bow.

HUNDREDS OF WORKERS – from riveters, plumbers, and electricians to painters, engineers, blacksmiths, and carpenters – are employed in a shipyard. The first iron ships were constructed in much the same way as skeleton-built wood ships (pp. 18–19). The internal structure of the ship was erected first and then the shell was fastened around it. The metal plates were even riveted together in much the same way as the planks of a wood boat (p. 19). And iron and steel ships were still built in the open air, as wood ships had been for centuries. But since 1945, welding has replaced riveting. Computers are now widely used to automate plate-cutting and welding, and many ships are built in sections, which are then fastened together. When the ship is finally launched, it hits the water as an empty metal shell. Then the work of "fitting out" – preparing the vessel for a lifetime at sea – begins.

ON THE STOCKS
To allow easy access and an easy launch, the hull of a ship under construction is held in place by wooden supports called stocks. This picture shows the luxurious liner *Aquitania* (pp. 54–57) in 1913. She was launched, stern first, into the Clyde River in Scotland a few weeks later.

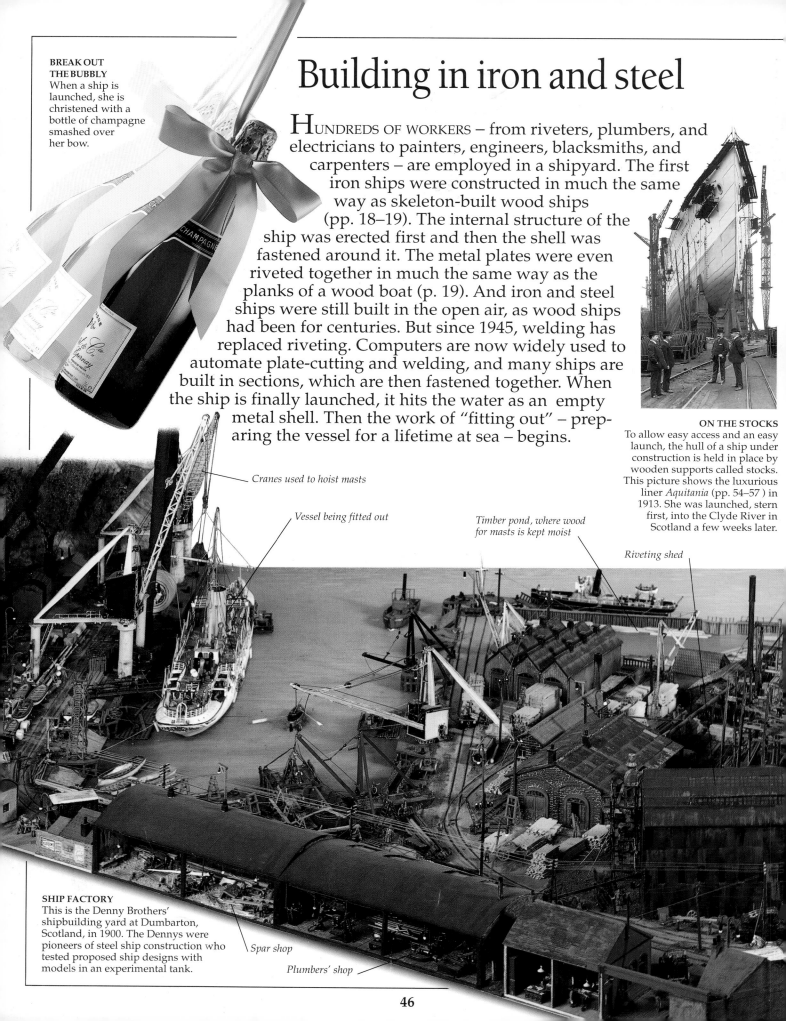

Cranes used to hoist masts

Vessel being fitted out

Timber pond, where wood for masts is kept moist

Riveting shed

SHIP FACTORY
This is the Denny Brothers' shipbuilding yard at Dumbarton, Scotland, in 1900. The Dennys were pioneers of steel ship construction who tested proposed ship designs with models in an experimental tank.

Spar shop

Plumbers' shop

RED-HOT RIVETS
These men are fastening hull plates together. Red-hot rivets are hammered through the drilled plates. A man on the inside of the hull then flattens out the rivet ends to keep them from coming out.

IRON WARRIOR
This is one half of the middle section of *Warrior*, Britain's first ironclad battleship. Inside a wood-and-iron shell, she has iron beams and brackets to support the decks. These irons beams not only are stronger than the old wood supports but also take up less space inside the ship.

METAL PEGS
These are some of the types of rivets used in shipbuilding to fasten together overlapping iron or steel plates.

ISAMBARD KINGDOM
The British engineer Isambard Kingdom Brunel designed and built three revolutionary ships in the mid 1800s. This picture shows him in the yard of the last one, the *Great Eastern* (p. 37), just before the second attempt to launch her. It was only on the seventh attempt, after three months and the death of a laborer, that the enormous ship was finally floated.

These metal frames on a building slipway are the beginnings of a large steamship

Walkway along wood scaffolding

Small steamer nearing completion

Metal bulkheads, which divide a ship into watertight compartments, have just been added to this steamer

Vacant building slipway

Frame-bending shed

Furnace shed

Furnace shed

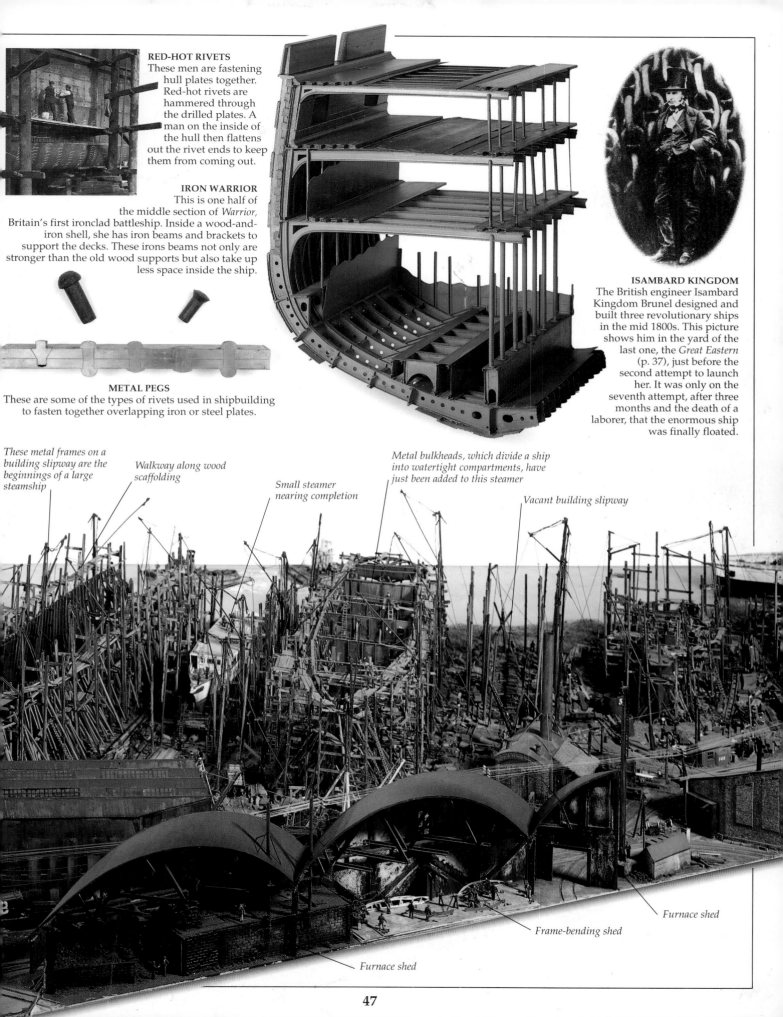

Tramping the seas

FLAGGING OUT
Because of heavy taxes in Europe and North America, 12 percent of the world's merchant ships are registered under the Panamian flag.

THOUGH AIRPLANES have taken passenger traffic away from ships, they have had little impact on the carrying of cargo. More than 95 percent of all international cargo is still transported by sea. Until recently, most cargo ships carried a wide range of goods. Early steamships were called "tramps" because they carried all kinds of cargo and chugged from port to port with no fixed route. There are still a few tramps today, but there are also many specialized vessels, built to carry just one type of cargo or perform one particular job. With rising fuel, crew, and cargo-handling costs, there is a continual drive to develop more efficient and economical ships.

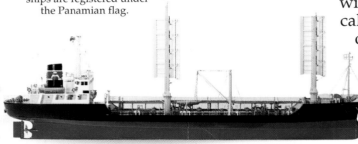

BACK TO SAILS
Launched in 1980, the Japanese *Shin Aitoku Maru* was the world's first motor tanker to be fitted with computer-controlled sails. Her fuel bill is about 10 percent less than a tanker of the same size with no sails.

COLD CARRIER
The Norwegian *Norman Lady* is built to carry 3,092,300 ft^3 (87,600 m^3) of natural gas in special spherical tanks. In order to take up less space, the gas is chilled to a temperature of -261°F (-163°C), when it forms a liquid. The nickel steel tanks are strong enough to withstand the enormous pressure and are completely insulated from the rest of the ship so the extreme cold does not cause the steel to fracture.

TRAMPING INTO THE RED SEA
The *Springwell* had a searchlight mounted at her bow to help her pass through the Suez Canal. At sea, the light would be shipped, or stored, and her cargo hatches would be covered with canvas tarpaulins. Until she was sunk by a torpedo in 1916, this tramp carried coal from Britain to bunker stations – places where ships could take on coal – all around the world. Miraculously, all her crew survived her sinking.

Poop deck, the third "island" on a three-island steamer

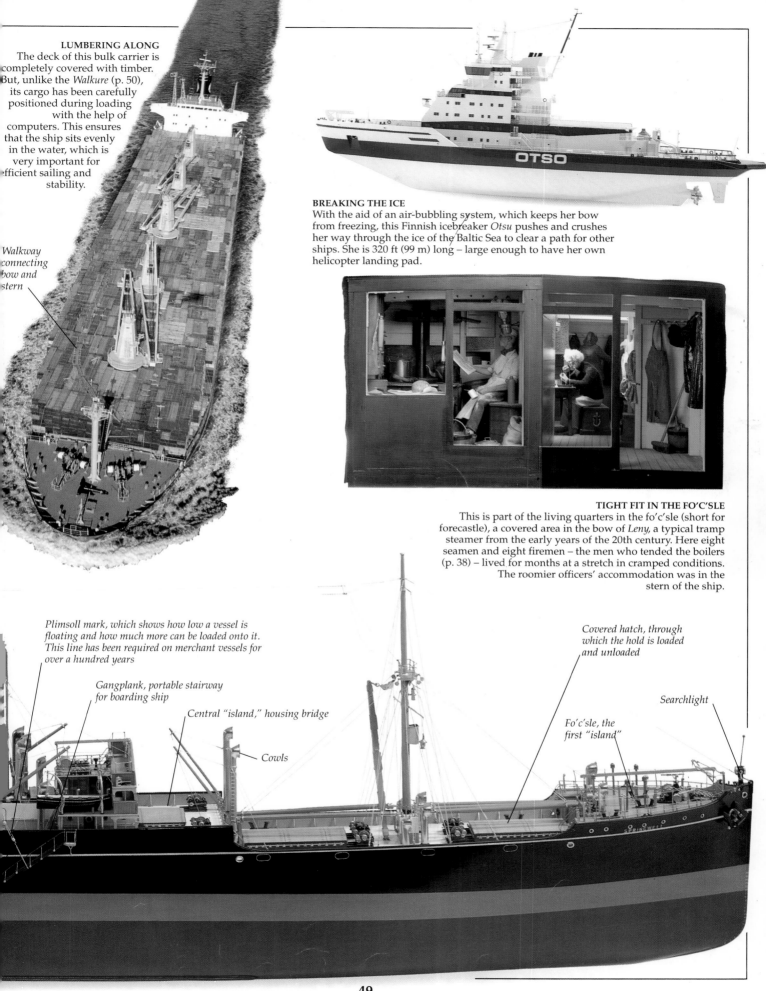

LUMBERING ALONG
The deck of this bulk carrier is completely covered with timber. But, unlike the *Walkure* (p. 50), its cargo has been carefully positioned during loading with the help of computers. This ensures that the ship sits evenly in the water, which is very important for efficient sailing and stability.

Walkway connecting bow and stern

BREAKING THE ICE
With the aid of an air-bubbling system, which keeps her bow from freezing, this Finnish icebreaker *Otsu* pushes and crushes her way through the ice of the Baltic Sea to clear a path for other ships. She is 320 ft (99 m) long – large enough to have her own helicopter landing pad.

TIGHT FIT IN THE FO'C'SLE
This is part of the living quarters in the fo'c'sle (short for forecastle), a covered area in the bow of *Leny*, a typical tramp steamer from the early years of the 20th century. Here eight seamen and eight firemen – the men who tended the boilers (p. 38) – lived for months at a stretch in cramped conditions. The roomier officers' accommodation was in the stern of the ship.

Plimsoll mark, which shows how low a vessel is floating and how much more can be loaded onto it. This line has been required on merchant vessels for over a hundred years

Gangplank, portable stairway for boarding ship

Central "island," housing bridge

Cowls

Covered hatch, through which the hold is loaded and unloaded

Searchlight

Fo'c'sle, the first "island"

In the dock

BEFORE THEY CAN TIE UP at the dock, most merchant ships have to be towed into port by tugs. They are then loaded or unloaded by cranes, as they have been since Roman times. The skylines of modern ports are dominated by huge steel cranes. Until recently, large numbers of people were employed on the docks to handle cargo, carefully loading and unloading ships before reloading the goods onto trains or trucks. But the increasing use of containers has drastically reduced the need for workers. And the growth in the size of ships – particularly tankers, which can have decks 1,000 ft (350 m) long and carry 330,000 tons of oil – means that fewer ports have the facilities to dock them.

Bridge

PUSHED AND PULLED
Off St. Croix island in the Caribbean, a huge supertanker is being moved into position by five tugs. As the size of tankers increases, there are fewer ports with deep enough water and long enough docks to take them. Many now tie up and unload at giant offshore mooring buoys.

Helicopter pad

TOTE THAT BALE
These dockers at Port Sudan are loading bales of cotton – Sudan's principal export – into a ship's hold (its cargo space).

OOPS!
Ships must be loaded carefully to keep them stable. This tramp, *Walkure*, took on too much coal in her port bunkers and rolled over. The timber on her deck damaged her masts and superstructure (the part of the ship above the main deck), but she didn't roll any further. After four days on her side in this position, she was righted again.

CLEVER PACKAGING
This is the container port at Hong Kong. Putting goods into standard-size containers has revolutionized cargo handling. Giant cranes lift the sealed containers off the ship and drop them on the shore or straight onto waiting trucks.

FENDING OFF

This rope fender is hung from the side of a boat to keep it from scraping against the dock or against other boats. Old tires do the same job.

FROM STEAMSHIP TO STEAM TRAIN

Most ports are well served by railroads. In this poster advertising the South Wales Docks near Cardiff, a steamship's cargo of timber is being loaded into the freight cars of a waiting steam train.

DOCKERS' TOOLS

Hooks like these are used to grab hold of packages swung to and from a ship by cranes.

AND ON THE INSIDE...

Even inside a container, goods must be packed in manageable units, like this Japanese tea chest.

1957
7013
鐘 牧 重
中國茶叶出口公司

ROPED TO THE DOCK

Ships (and ropes) may have gotten a lot bigger, but the basic method of tying them to bollards, or posts, on the dock has not changed for centuries.

Wheelhouse

DANUBE VI

Towing rope

Rudder

Propeller in well

MOVER OF THE MIGHTY

In restricted waterways like ports, large ships cannot maneuver easily and must rely on tugs to tow them. This one, *Danube VI*, worked on the Thames River in London in the 1930s. Modern towing tugs are very similar, with a large hook (not shown here) attached to the end of the tow rope and an unobstructed deck at the stern. Liners like the *Mauretania* (pp. 54–55) had to be moved by six tugs.

DOWN IN THE HOLD

The cargo hold of this freighter is packed with small loose bundles of cocoa, which must be loaded and unloaded by dockers.

ANCHORS AWAY

A ship at rest is buffetted by winds, tides, and currents. Whether stopping for the night or waiting for a berth in port, the captain drops an anchor to fix the vessel to the seabed. The first anchors were stones or baskets full of rocks. Modern anchors come in many shapes and sizes.

Plow anchor for yachts

Stockless anchor, carried by most metal ships

"Fisherman's" anchor, used for wood craft

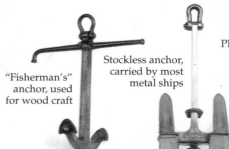

On the bridge

THE BRIDGE of this firefighting boat houses the vessel's navigational and steering instruments as well as the controls for its engines and water pumps, all in one small area. Like all bridges, it is positioned for good visibility. Old sailing ships were controlled from a raised deck on the stern, the quarterdeck. But the bridge on a steam or motorized ship is farther forward, so that the people at the controls are well clear of the smoke from the funnels and can see where they are going.

PORT LIGHT
A red light is always hung on the port side (left as you face the bow) of a ship, while a green light is hung on the starboard (right). In fog or darkness, these lights tell other ships which way a vessel is going.

DEAD SLOW AHEAD
With a wire and chain mechanism, this "telegraph" from a large steamship was used to transmit orders from the bridge to the engine room, where there was a similar dial (p. 38). The fireboat does not need a telegraph because the men on the bridge have direct control of the engines.

Compass gimbal, with metal balls which counteract magnetism of steel boat

Switches used for sending fire-fighting orders to engine room

Wheel to turn rudder and steer boat

Pump gauges

Imperial Russian eagle

Lamp

Compass and card sit in here

COMPASS HOLDER
This is the "binnacle," or housing, for the compass card shown on the left. The brass top is gimballed, or pivoted, so that it will roll as the ship rolls, thus keeping the compass flat. At the very top is a lamp to illuminate the compass at night.

WAYFINDER
This is a compass card from a 19th-century ship of the Russian Imperial Navy. On most land compasses, the needle moves around the card. But on a maritime compass, the needle is fixed to the underside of the card so that both move.

Green starboard light, to indicate right side of boat

Radar with shield to keep out daylight

The "Turk's head", a knot tied around one of the wheel's spokes; in this position, the rudder is in line with the hull and the boat is going straight ahead

Port and starboard engine throttles and gears, to allow boat to maneuver in tight spots

Panel with engine gauges

Compass

Rudder angle indicator

Luxurious liners

As STEAMSHIPS DEVELOPED, they could travel between continents faster than any vessel under sail. Special ships were built to carry large numbers of passengers across the Atlantic and Pacific. These ships were called liners, because they worked regular lines (routes). The Golden Age of the liner was in the 1920s and 1930s, when enormous, luxurious ships sailed the world. For the richest passengers, who traveled first class, these ships rivaled the best hotels on land. There was great competition among the shipping companies to provide the quickest service across the Atlantic. The fastest ship was said to hold the "Blue Riband." The most successful company was the British Cunard Line, which built a number of record-breaking ships. But by the 1950s, liners could not compete with jet airliners for speed or price. One by one, most of them have been retired and broken up for scrap.

GERMAN CHAMPION
The *Bremen* was one of many fast German liners which rivaled Cunard's ships for the Blue Riband. She succeeded in capturing it from the *Mauretania* on her maiden (first) voyage in 1929.

COFFEE SHOP
This is the elegant veranda café on Canadian Pacific's *Empress of Australia* in the 1930s.

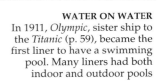

WATER ON WATER
In 1911, *Olympic*, sister ship to the *Titanic* (p. 59), became the first liner to have a swimming pool. Many liners had both indoor and outdoor pools

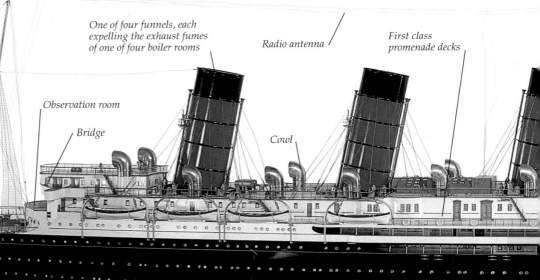

One of four funnels, each expelling the exhaust fumes of one of four boiler rooms

Radio antenna

First class promenade decks

Observation room

Bridge

Cowl

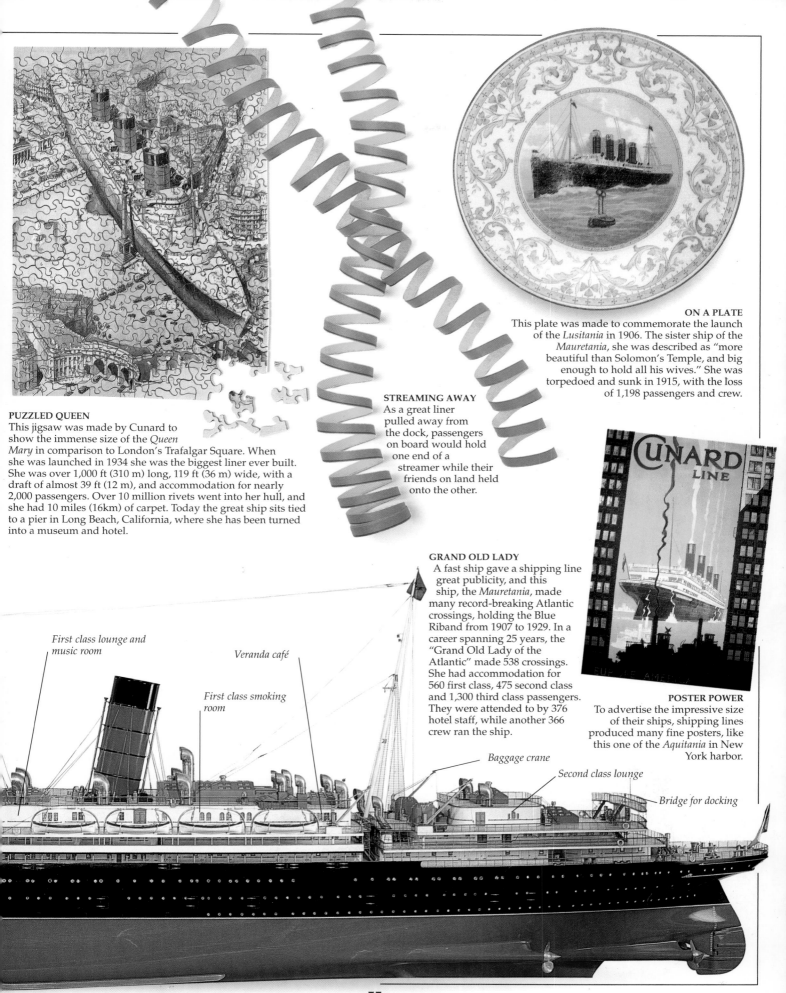

PUZZLED QUEEN
This jigsaw was made by Cunard to
show the immense size of the *Queen
Mary* in comparison to London's Trafalgar Square. When
she was launched in 1934 she was the biggest liner ever built.
She was over 1,000 ft (310 m) long, 119 ft (36 m) wide, with a
draft of almost 39 ft (12 m), and accommodation for nearly
2,000 passengers. Over 10 million rivets went into her hull, and
she had 10 miles (16km) of carpet. Today the great ship sits tied
to a pier in Long Beach, California, where she has been turned
into a museum and hotel.

ON A PLATE
This plate was made to commemorate the launch
of the *Lusitania* in 1906. The sister ship of the
Mauretania, she was described as "more
beautiful than Solomon's Temple, and big
enough to hold all his wives." She was
torpedoed and sunk in 1915, with the loss
of 1,198 passengers and crew.

STREAMING AWAY
As a great liner
pulled away from
the dock, passengers
on board would hold
one end of a
streamer while their
friends on land held
onto the other.

GRAND OLD LADY
A fast ship gave a shipping line
great publicity, and this
ship, the *Mauretania*, made
many record-breaking Atlantic
crossings, holding the Blue
Riband from 1907 to 1929. In a
career spanning 25 years, the
"Grand Old Lady of the
Atlantic" made 538 crossings.
She had accommodation for
560 first class, 475 second class
and 1,300 third class passengers.
They were attended to by 376
hotel staff, while another 366
crew ran the ship.

POSTER POWER
To advertise the impressive size
of their ships, shipping lines
produced many fine posters, like
this one of the *Aquitania* in New
York harbor.

*First class lounge and
music room*

Veranda café

*First class smoking
room*

Baggage crane

Second class lounge

Bridge for docking

Continued on next page

Continued from previous page

N.Y.K. LINE

M

DESTINATION

M.S."   MARU"
S.S.

CLASS

BAGGAGE ROOM

PRINTED IN JAPAN

LINER LUGGAGE
This is a baggage ticket of the Nippon Yusen Kaisha Line, or "the Japanese Mail Steamship Company," which ran from 1885 to 1960. It took many Japanese immigrants to Hawaii.

O.S.K. Line

OSAKA SHOSEN KAISHA

JAPANESE GIANT
Founded in the 1880s, the OSK line is now part of Mitsui-OSK, second only to P&O as the largest shipping line in the world.

SAFETY AT SEA
Like all modern liners, the Italian Line's *Michelangelo* has lifeboats for all her passengers and crew, a total of nearly 2,000 people. Rigorous safety standards were introduced after the *Titanic* disaster (p. 59), and all passengers must do lifeboat drills.

GENTLEMEN PREFER BLONDES
In a scene from this popular 1953 film, actress Marilyn Monroe looks through a porthole. These round windows weaken the steel structure of a liner much less than rectangular ones.

P&O MENU

LUNCH ON A LINER
This menu was printed for the British liner company Peninsular and Orient (P&O), which specialized in travel to the Far East.

CABIN COMFORTS
Maple paneling and a pair of portholes are among the features of a first class double cabin on board the *Empress of Canada*. Launched in 1960, this Canadian Pacific liner could carry 200 first class and 856 tourist class passengers.

Coffee pot

Tea pot

Hot water jug

TEA AND COFFEE
This coffee and tea service was used on Orient Line ships sailing to and from Australia in the 1960s.

LUXURY CRUISER
Sailing in style continues today on luxury cruise ships like the *Crown Princess* , launched in 1989. These ships are built for vacationers, not travelers.

DUTCH PRIDE
Built in 1929, the *Statendam* was the flagship of the Holland-America Line. This company's reputation for cleanliness earned it the nickname "the Spotless Fleet."

FIRST SIGHT
Since it was erected in 1886, the Statue of Liberty has greeted passengers arriving by boat in New York harbor.

To a new life

The cheapest accommodations of the great liners were largely occupied by emigrants leaving their homelands to make new lives in the United States, Canada, Australia, and New Zealand. Emigration to North America had begun in the 17th century. Many of the first settlers left Europe because of religious or political persecution. So did later emigrants, like those from Russia and Eastern Europe. Others, from Ireland and Italy in particular, left to escape famine and poverty. Still others came to the "New World" – the Americas – because it offered more opportunities than the old. Emigration continues today, on a smaller scale but for much the same reasons.

OLD AND NEW
On this poster, the *Mauretania* steams past a sailing ship. While it might take weeks to sail across the Atlantic, the liner could make the crossing in 5 days.

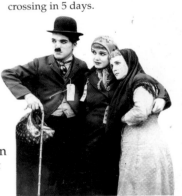

Cross of St. George, the English flag

Square top and main sails

Lateen mizzen sail

EARLY ARRIVALS
This tiny ship, only about 125 ft (40m) long, arrived in America on November 11, 1620, having left England 67 days before. It was the *Mayflower,* and on board were 102 Puritans, members of a religious sect who had fled persecution at home. They founded the first permanent European colony in what is now the United States.

TRAMPING ACROSS THE OCEAN
In the short film *The Immigrant,* actor Charlie Chaplin plays a tramp on board a steamship bound for America. Chaplin himself had left the poverty of a London slum and made his career and fortune in the United States.

BOAT PEOPLE
Political events sometimes force people to take great risks in leaving their home countries. These Vietnamese refugees have paid large sums of money for a dangerous passage on a small boat. With luck, they will reach Hong Kong.

LEAVING HOME
On the wharf at Genoa in 1901, Italians who have fled war in the north wait with their few possessions to board steamers bound for America.

TURNED AWAY
After 1945, many Jews left Europe for Palestine. The people on one crowded ship were turned away by the British authorities and had to return to Germany. This incident caused an international outcry and was featured in a 1961 film. Like the ship, the film was called *Exodus,* which means leaving.

S.O.S. (Save Our Souls!)

THREE DOTS, THREE DASHES, AND THREE DOTS is the Morse code signal for S.O.S. – short for Save Our Souls, a desperate plea for help from other ships or the shore. Every maritime nation has a rescue service and maintains lighthouses and lightships to warn sailors of dangerous rocks and shallows. Professional sailors take all the precautions they can. Ships are equipped with radios, radar, depth sounders, and emergency flares, and since the *Titanic* disaster they are obliged to carry lifeboats and life jackets for all on board. But the sea has not been conquered, and its bed is still littered with wrecks. Ships go down every year; some even vanish without trace. And because ships are now larger than ever before and carry more dangerous cargo, disasters can be much greater.

CASTAWAY
Robinson Crusoe was based on the true story of Alexander Selkirk, who was abandoned on a Pacific island in 1704.

TO THE RESCUE
The popular beaches of Australia are patrolled by lifeguards, who are always ready to rescue swimmers or surfers who get into difficulties. Their rowboats are specially designed to ride over the high surf.

SEA DEVIL
Mermaids were considered bad omens. A sailor who thought he saw one may have really been looking at a mammal called a dugong, an ocean-going relative of the elephant.

Hand-held flares

Foghorn

FLARES AND WAILS
This foghorn uses a a cylinder of compressed air to make an ear-piercing noise. As well as warning of a ship's presence, it can be used to signal simple messages. Flares are distress signals and help to guide searching rescue craft.

BELLOWING OUT
Fog is a great danger at sea because it obscures rocks, lighthouses, and other ships. The handle on this portable foghorn pumps a set of bellows to produce a wailing sound, which alerts other vessels to the ship's presence.

ABANDONED SHIP
In November 1872, a month after she left New York, the *Mary Celeste* was found drifting in the Atlantic with no one on board. Her tender (p. 6) was missing and she looked as if she had been abandoned in a great hurry. There are many theories as to what happened. There may have been a mutiny, with the crew turning against their captain. Or the crew may have fled because they feared her cargo of alcohol was about to explode. Either way, no one knows what happened to the 10 people on board, which included a two-year-old girl.

RESCUE THE RESCUERS
British lifeboat men risk their lives to save other sailors, but because they are called out when the sea is most dangerous, disaster can strike them too.

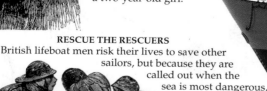

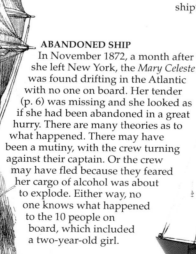

KENTISH KNOCK

20

LIGHTSHIP
A lightship is anchored in treacherous spots where a lighthouse cannot be built. This one is moored in the North Sea 20 miles (32 km) off the English coast. A crew of seven lives on board. Her light is 40 ft (12 m) above sea level and can be seen from 24 miles (38 km) away. It is a "dumb" ship, meaning that it has no engine and had to be towed to its position on the Kentish Knock, a dangerous sandbank.

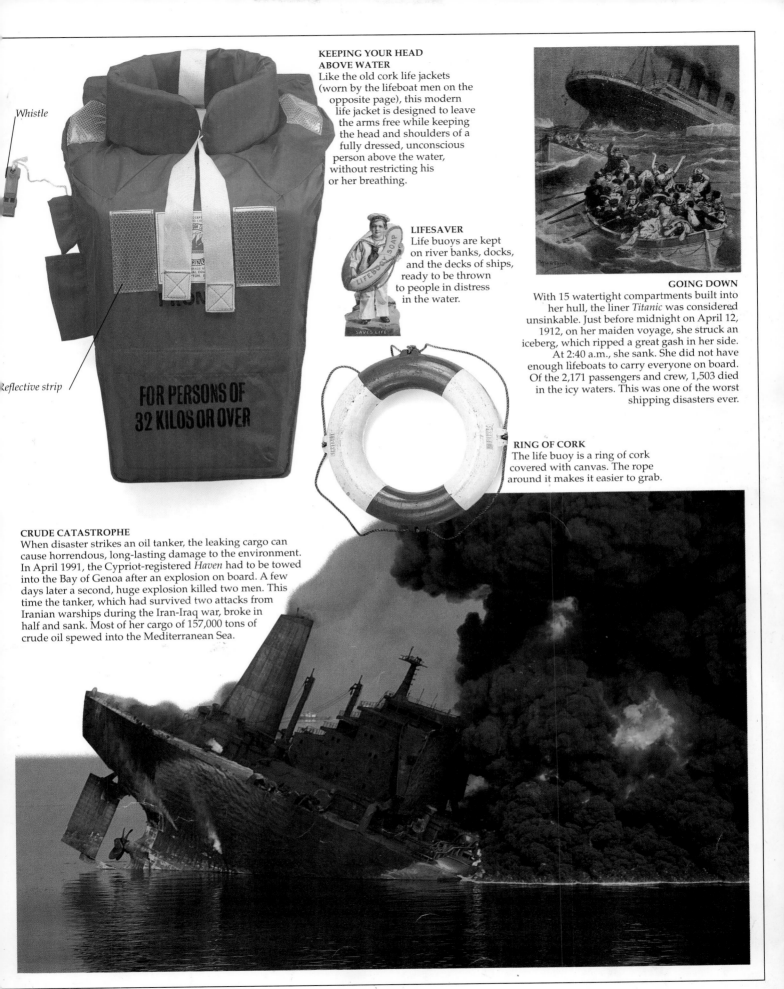

Whistle

Reflective strip

KEEPING YOUR HEAD ABOVE WATER
Like the old cork life jackets (worn by the lifeboat men on the opposite page), this modern life jacket is designed to leave the arms free while keeping the head and shoulders of a fully dressed, unconscious person above the water, without restricting his or her breathing.

LIFESAVER
Life buoys are kept on river banks, docks, and the decks of ships, ready to be thrown to people in distress in the water.

FOR PERSONS OF 32 KILOS OR OVER

GOING DOWN
With 15 watertight compartments built into her hull, the liner *Titanic* was considered unsinkable. Just before midnight on April 12, 1912, on her maiden voyage, she struck an iceberg, which ripped a great gash in her side. At 2:40 a.m., she sank. She did not have enough lifeboats to carry everyone on board. Of the 2,171 passengers and crew, 1,503 died in the icy waters. This was one of the worst shipping disasters ever.

RING OF CORK
The life buoy is a ring of cork covered with canvas. The rope around it makes it easier to grab.

CRUDE CATASTROPHE
When disaster strikes an oil tanker, the leaking cargo can cause horrendous, long-lasting damage to the environment. In April 1991, the Cypriot-registered *Haven* had to be towed into the Bay of Genoa after an explosion on board. A few days later a second, huge explosion killed two men. This time the tanker, which had survived two attacks from Iranian warships during the Iran-Iraq war, broke in half and sank. Most of her cargo of 157,000 tons of crude oil spewed into the Mediterranean Sea.

Sailing at speed

WINGED VICTOR
In 1983, this secret, revolutionary keel helped *Australia II* to become the first sailboat to capture the America's Cup from the Americans.

IN 1851 the New York Yacht Club's *America* (p. 7) beat the 15 best sailing yachts in Britain in a race around the Isle of Wight, off the south coast of England. The victorious club issued a challenge to the rest of the world's sailors, offering the cup they had won to any sailboat that could beat *America*. So began the most famous sailboat race of all, the America's Cup. Sailboat races were being held two centuries before this. The first yacht club was founded in 1720, at Cork, Ireland. At first sailing was the sport of the very wealthy. Even today, the sailboats that fight for the America's Cup and the Whitbread Round the World Race cost millions of dollars. A major industry devotes millions more to the search for faster, more efficient sailboats, testing new materials and designs. This is profitable because sailboat racing is now enjoyed by more and more people. There are many relatively cheap, mass-produced sailboats on the market. Some of these are raced against each other. Others are taken out to sea for the pure pleasure of sailing.

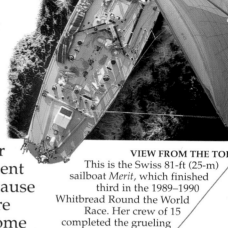

VIEW FROM THE TOP
This is the Swiss 81-ft (25-m) sailboat *Merit*, which finished third in the 1989–1990 Whitbread Round the World Race. Her crew of 15 completed the grueling circumnavigation in just over 69 days at sea.

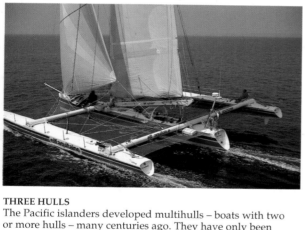

THREE HULLS
The Pacific islanders developed multihulls – boats with two or more hulls – many centuries ago. They have only been used in the West for offshore racing since the 1960s. This is *Elf Aquitaine III*, a French high-speed trimaran – a boat with three hulls. It is very stable and cannot roll over, though in the wrong conditions it may turn stern over bow.

Backstay

Wheel

Life buoy

Spinnaker sheet

Registration number –
the letter "K" indicates
that the boat is registered
in Britain

Batten to
stiffen sail

Mainsail, made
(like jib) of a
synthetic material
called Dacron

Mast, made of
lightweight alloy

Genoa, a large
kind of jib

Shroud

Spreader

Spinnaker,
made of
lightweight nylon

IN NEED OF A TRIM
The spinnaker (p. 23) is
making this Sigma 38
sailboat heel to starboard. This
can be cured by altering course
slightly, or by moving the weight of
the crew to the windward side. Both
the jib, which has become tangled, and
the mainsail, which is flapping, need
trimming, or adjusting. None of these
difficulties are too serious, however. Sailboats
like this are very seaworthy and rarely
capsize. They bring the
excitement of sailboat racing
(and gentle cruising) to many more
people than can afford an
international racing sailboat.

Learning the ropes

YOU CAN LEARN TO SAIL in a weekend. If you do, you may well spend the rest of your life perfecting your technique. There are now countless sailing clubs around the world – on lakes and by the sea. Sailing is becoming more and more popular both as a serious sport and as a pastime, offering not only challenge and excitement but also good exercise in the fresh air. To be a good competitive sailor, you must be very fit. It is not a dangerous sport, provided simple rules on safety and clothing are followed. Like any other sport, the best way to learn the basic points and skills is to take lessons. There are many organizations that run sailing schools, and hundreds of different types of small boats. Many people start to sail in simple boats like the one-person Optimist and then gradually move on to bigger and faster boats. Boats without decks used for pleasure sailing are usually called dinghies (from an Indian word for boat). The first dinghies were made of wood, but today most are built of molded plastic, which means they are sturdy and do not need much maintenance. Dinghies can be expensive to buy, but many clubs rent them out.

DRESSED TO GET WET
Even on the warmest day it is possible to get very cold and wet when sailing. It is important to dress properly for the sport.

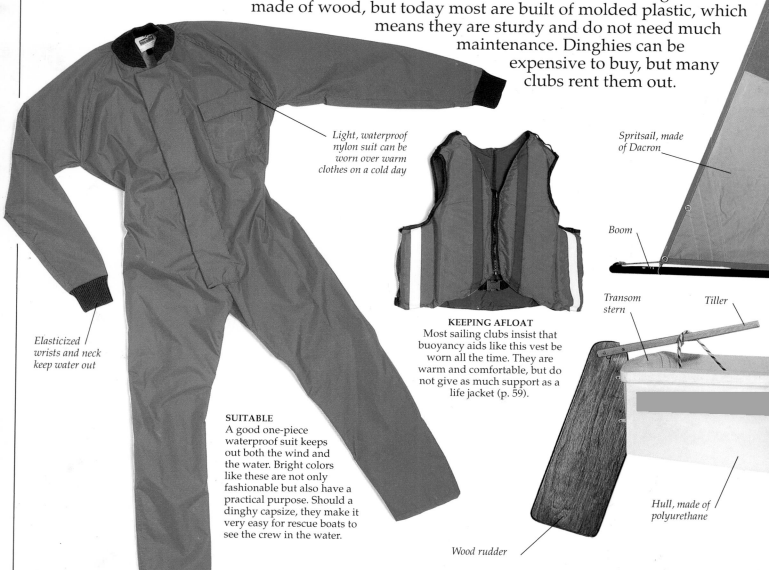

Light, waterproof nylon suit can be worn over warm clothes on a cold day

Elasticized wrists and neck keep water out

Spritsail, made of Dacron

Boom

Transom stern

Tiller

KEEPING AFLOAT
Most sailing clubs insist that buoyancy aids like this vest be worn all the time. They are warm and comfortable, but do not give as much support as a life jacket (p. 59).

SUITABLE
A good one-piece waterproof suit keeps out both the wind and the water. Bright colors like these are not only fashionable but also have a practical purpose. Should a dinghy capsize, they make it very easy for rescue boats to see the crew in the water.

Hull, made of polyurethane

Wood rudder

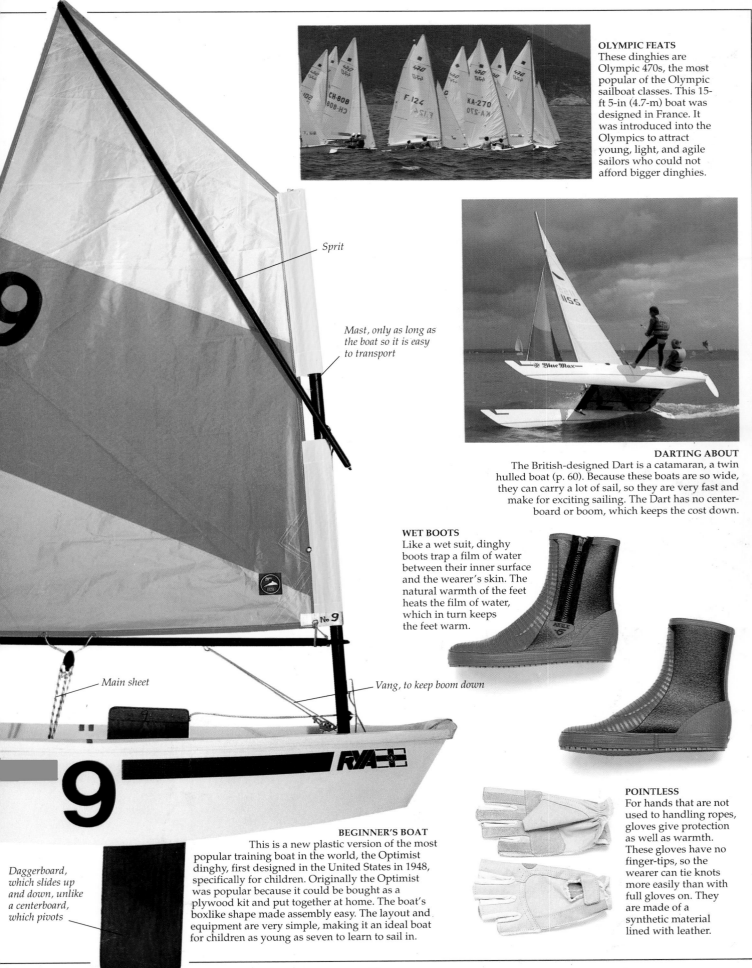

Sprit

Mast, only as long as
the boat so it is easy
to transport

OLYMPIC FEATS
These dinghies are
Olympic 470s, the most
popular of the Olympic
sailboat classes. This 15-
ft 5-in (4.7-m) boat was
designed in France. It
was introduced into the
Olympics to attract
young, light, and agile
sailors who could not
afford bigger dinghies.

DARTING ABOUT
The British-designed Dart is a catamaran, a twin
hulled boat (p. 60). Because these boats are so wide,
they can carry a lot of sail, so they are very fast and
make for exciting sailing. The Dart has no centerboard or boom, which keeps the cost down.

WET BOOTS
Like a wet suit, dinghy
boots trap a film of water
between their inner surface
and the wearer's skin. The
natural warmth of the feet
heats the film of water,
which in turn keeps
the feet warm.

Main sheet

Vang, to keep boom down

POINTLESS
For hands that are not
used to handling ropes,
gloves give protection
as well as warmth.
These gloves have no
finger-tips, so the
wearer can tie knots
more easily than with
full gloves on. They
are made of a
synthetic material
lined with leather.

BEGINNER'S BOAT
This is a new plastic version of the most
popular training boat in the world, the Optimist
dinghy, first designed in the United States in 1948,
specifically for children. Originally the Optimist
was popular because it could be bought as a
plywood kit and put together at home. The boat's
boxlike shape made assembly easy. The layout and
equipment are very simple, making it an ideal boat
for children as young as seven to learn to sail in.

Daggerboard,
which slides up
and down, unlike
a centerboard,
which pivots

Index

A

America's Cup 60
anchor 35, 43, 51
animal skins 6, 9, 10-11
Archimedes' screw 38

B

barges 21, 24, 32, 33, 34
bark 6
bark boats 12-13
battleship 47
Bayeux Tapestry 17
Becchi, Antonio 7
biremes 20
bladders 9
Blue Riband 54, 55
Bluebeard 29
boatbuilding 17, 18-19
Bogart, Humphrey 36
boom 7, 15, 22, 27, 32, 33, 62, 63
bow 7, 15, 20, 21, 32, 33, 46, 48, 49, 60
bowsprit 25, 27, 41
bridge 52, 54, 55
brig 26, 27
Brunel, Isambard Kingdom 47
bulk carrier 7
bulkheads 47
bull boats 10

C

caballito 21
canal boats 34, 35
cannon 20, 28
canoes 10, 13, 14, 16, 32, 33
cargo ships 7, 29, 34, 48-49, 50-51
catamaran 63
centerboard 23, 35, 63
Chaplin, Charlie 57
clippers 40, 41
coble 17
cog ship 17, 24
Columbus, Christopher 26
compass 52, 53
container ships 6, 50
Cook, James 26
coracles 10, 11, 21
curragh 10

D

da Gama, Vasco 26
deck 41, 49, 62
dhows 25
diesel power 45
dinghies 62-63
docks 50-51
dory 43
dugout canoes 14-15, 21

E

edge-joined boats 16, 17
engine room 52
Ericsson, John 38
Ericsson, Leif 17

F

ferries 6, 16
figureheads 32-33
fire-fighting boat 52
fishing 6, 8, 9, 10, 12, 14, 42-45; boats 15, 16, 17, 21, 25, 32, 33, 42-45; nets 44
fitting out 46
flagship 56
floats 6, 15, 43
fo'c'sle 49
foghorn 58
Frederick, Prince 33
freighter 51
funnels 52

G

galleon 15
galleys 20, 21
gangplank 49
George II 33
gondola 21, 32, 34
gun deck 28
gunwale 10

H

hammock 28
harpooning 11, 30-31

heeling 23
Hepburn, Katherine 36
Heyerdahl, Thor 9
Hopkins, Frances Ann 12
Hudson's Bay Company 12
hulk 17, 24
hull 7, 14, 15, 27, 47, 53, 54, 60, 62

I

icebreaker 49
inland boats 34-35
iron ships 41, 46-47

J

jib sail 23, 24, 27, 61
jibing 22
jigger 40
Jolly Roger 29
junks 24, 34, 35

K

kayaks 10, 11, 21
keel 7, 17, 19, 23, 34, 35, 60
Kent, William 33

L

lapstrake boats 16, 17, 18, 31
lateen sail 20, 21, 25, 57
launching 26, 46
leeboards 34, 35
lifeboats 56, 58, 59
life jackets 58, 59, 62
lighthouses 58
Lincoln, Abraham 32
liners 36, 38, 54-57
log boats 6, 8, 14, 15, 16, 18
longships 17, 24
lugsail 24, 25, 42

M

mainsail 23, 24, 41, 57, 61
merchant ships 21, 27, 32, 40-41, 50
mess 28
mizzen mast 25, 40, 57
Monroe, Marilyn 56
Morgan, Captain 29

Morse code 58
motor vessels 32, 48, 52

N

navigation 52
Noah's Ark 16

O

oars 8, 10, 17, 20-21, 43
oil tankers 7, 50, 59
oruwa 15
outboard motor 39, 43
outriggers 14-15, 21, 45

P

packet steamer 37
paddle wheelers 36, 37, 38
paddles 10, 20, 21, 30, 42
papyrus rafts 8
paracils 10, 11
Pettit Smith, Francis 38
pirates 21, 28, 29
plank boats 6, 13, 14, 15, 16-19, 46
plastic 12, 13, 21, 43, 62, 63
Plimsoll mark 49
poop deck 48
pooping 27
port light 52
port side 7, 21, 39, 53
porthole 56
powerboat 7
proa 21
propellers 7, 36, 37, 38-39, 51
prow 16
punting 6, 20, 34

Q

quarterdeck 52
quffa 11

R

radar 53, 58
rafts 6, 8-9
rattan 16
reed boat 21
rigging 22, 25, 41

riverboat 21, 36, 38
Roberts, Bartholomew 29
rowing 20, 31, 43, 58
rudder 7, 14, 17, 21, 25, 39, 45, 51, 52, 53, 62
rudder mounting 35
rum 28

S

sailboats 7, 14, 60
sailing 22-23, 28-29, 60-61, 62-63
ships 6, 26-27, 33, 40, 41, 57
trawlers 43
sailmaking 26
sailors 28-29, 30, 58
sails 7, 13, 24-25, 31, 33, 35, 37, 43, 61, 63; jib 23; lateen 20, 21, 25; leaf 15, 30; main 23, 41, 57; settee 25; spinnaker 23; square 6, 20, 24, 27, 40, 41, 57; studding 27
sampans 34, 35
schooner 43
screws 38, 39
sculling 21
seine net 44
Selkirk, Alexander 58
sheets 22, 60, 63
shell construction 18
ship 6, 32, 41
shipbuilding 46-47
shipping lines 55, 56
shrouds 7, 22, 23, 41, 61
skeleton construction 18, 46
slavery 28, 29
spar 23
spinnaker sail 23, 60, 61
spritsail 14, 24, 62
square sails 6, 20, 24, 27, 40, 41, 57
starboard light 52, 53
starboard side 7, 39, 52, 61
stays 7, 22
staysails 24, 35
steam engines 36-39, 45
steamships 32, 35, 36-37, 40, 41, 47, 48, 51, 52, 54, 57
steel ships 33, 46-47
stern 7, 33, 49, 60, 62
rudder 35
trawling 44, 45

sternwheelers 36
strakes 19
studding sail 27
supertankers 39, 50

T

tacking 22
tankers 48, 50
tar 10, 11, 27
tea clippers 41
tiller 7, 22, 33, 35, 62
topsail 24, 27
trading ships 17, 24, 25, 28, 40
tramp ships 48, 49, 50
trawlers 42, 43, 44-45
trimaran 60
triremes 20
tugs 7, 50, 51
Tutankhamen, King 8

W

warships 20, 21, 28, 32, 33
whaling 30-31
wheelhouse 52
Whitbread Round the World Race 60
William the Conqueror 17
windsurfer 8
wooden craft 18, 46, 51, 62

Y

yachts 7, 51, 60-61
yard 7, 22, 25, 26, 41

Acknowledgments

Dorling Kindersley would like to thank:
David Spence, Caroline Roberts, Keith Percival and Barry Cash of the National Maritime Museum, Greenwich; David Goddard, Peter Crutwell, Christine O'Neill and Liz Hyde of the Exeter Maritime Museum; Christi Graham and Nick Nicholls of the British Museum, London; John Lepine of the Science Museum, London; Tony O'Connor for the tools for p. 19; Richard Boots for coming out in the rain to allow us to photograph his fireboat for pp. 52-53; Paulene Lashmare of the Royal Yachting Association for providing the training dinghy on pp. 60-61; Colin Merrett of Racing Sailboats for the clothes on pp. 60-61; Christian Sévigny, Liz Sephton, Sarah Cowley and Cheryl Telfer for design assistance; Claire Gillard and Helena Spiteri for editorial assistance; Céline Carez for her energetic research.

Illustrations Rob Shone
Index Jane Parker

Picture credits
t=top, b=bottom, c=center, l=left, r=right
All sport: 63/Vandystadt: 9cl, 11tl.
Ardea/Hans Dossenbach: 38cl.
Becken of Cowes: 63cr.
Biblioteca Marciana, Venice: 17crt.
Bibliotheque Nationale: 13c.
British Library: 12tr
Courtesy of the Trustees of the British Museum: 6tl, 20b.
British Waterways Archives: 32c.

J Allan Cash: 7tr, 13bl, 32cl.
Christel Clear: 60-1.
Cunard Postcards copyright 1990 Marine Art Posters, Hull: 55cr, 57tr.
Michael Dent: 32tl.
E.T.Archive: 7br, 15cl, 29ctr, 57cb, 59tr.
Editions Albert Rene/Goscinny-Uderzo: 21cl.
Mary Evans Picture Library: 7cl, 14tl, 44br, 45br, 58tl, 58cl.
Werner Foreman Archive: 30clb, 31cl.
Giraudon: 9tl.
Susan Griggs: 10cl, 10bl.
Sonia Halliday: 16bl
Robert Harding: 8br, 9tr, 25cr, 43cr.
Michael Holford: 11crb, 17tl, 17br, 20tr, 35bl.
Hulton Picture Co: 36br.
Hutchinson Library: 25tl, 43c.
Image bank/Jay Masiel: 40cl,/A. Boccaccio 51tr,/G Heisler 51bl.
Eric Kentley/National Maritime Museum: 10br, 16cr.
Kobal Collection 34tr/ 56tr, 57cr, 57br.
Magnum/Bruno Barbey: 8tl, /Burt Glinn 21tl, 32cr,/Ian Berry 57bl.
Mansell Collection: 24tl, 34cr, 37cb, 47tl, 47tr.

Ministry of Tourism, Old Fort William: 13tl, 13tc.
National Archives of Canada (Hopkins c-2771): 12b.
National Gallery of Canada: 13br
National Maritime Museum: 11crt,16tr, 26br, 27tl 27cr, 28bl, 28c, 28tr,28br, 29cr, 29br, 33c, 38bl, 39tr, 39cr, 41cl, 41b, 42b, 42tl, 43tl, 45tr, 46tr, 50bl, 50cr, 54c, 55tl, 56tl.
Robert Opie Collection: 54tl, 54cl, 54cr, 57ct, 59c.
Otago Museum, New Zealand: 40tl
Pitchall Picture Library/Cliff Webb: 8cl, 22-3, 60tl, 60cl, 60tr, 62tl.
Pictor International: 34cb.
Popperphoto: 9bl. Princess Cruises: 56br.
Ronan Picture Library: 27br, 36tl.
Science Museum, London: 21cr.
Select Photos: 59br
Smithsonian Institution: 13tr.
Archives Unit, University of Liverpool: 37tl.
Welsh Industrial and Maritime Museum, Cardiff: 51tl.
Zefa: 6c, 15cr, 42tr, 43tr, 49tl, 50tl, 50br, 56tr, 58cl.